To

From

As you take this journey we call life, may these words of encouragement from *Our Daily Bread* help guide your steps and put hope in your heart. We trust that you'll feel the assurance of God's presence and the comfort of His peace along the way.

© 2015 by Our Daily Bread Ministries. All rights reserved.

Discovery House is affiliated with Our Daily Bread Ministries, Grand Rapids, Michigan.

Requests for permission to quote from this book should be directed to: Permissions Department, Discovery House, P.O. Box 3566, Grand Rapids, MI 49501, or contact us by e-mail at permissionsdept@dhp.org.

All Scripture quotations, unless otherwise indicated, are taken from the Holy Bible, New International Version®, NIV®. Copyright ©1973, 1978, 1984, 2011 by Biblica, Inc.™ Used by permission of Zondervan. All rights reserved worldwide. www.zondervan.com. The "NIV" and "New International Version" are trademarks registered in the United States Patent and Trademark Office by Biblica, Inc.™

Contributing Writers: Henry G. Bosch (HGB); Dave Branon (DB); Dave Burnham (DBH); Anne Cetas (AC); Bill Crowder (BC); Dennis DeHaan (DD); Mart DeHaan (MD); M. R. DeHaan (MRD); Richard DeHaan (RD); David C. Egner (DCE); Dennis Fisher (DF); Vernon Grounds (VG); Tim Gustafson (TG); C. P. Hia (CPH); Cindy Hess Kasper (CHK); Randy Kilgore (RK); Albert Lee (AL); Julie Ackerman Link (JAL); David C. McCasland (DCM); Keila Ochoa (KO); Jerry Paulson (JP); David H. Roper (DHR); Haddon Robinson (HR); Jennifer Benson Schuldt (JBS); Joe Stowell (JS); Marion Stroud (MS); Herbert Vander Lugt (HVL); Paul Van Gorder (PVG); Marvin Williams (MW); Joanie Yoder (JY).

Design by Stan Myers

Photography: Thinkstock and Wikimedia Commons

Printed in China
First printing in 2015

JANUARY 1

Be very careful, then, how you live. —Ephesians 5:15

My wife, Martie, is a savvy shopper. At the grocery, she doesn't grab the first gallon of milk. To get the freshest milk, she gets the one with the latest "use by" date.

Our lives are marked by "use by" dates—but we don't know when we'll take our last breath on this planet. Therefore, shouldn't we work hard to capture the moments we've been given? Shouldn't we love more deeply, forgive more quickly, listen more carefully, and speak more affirmingly? Paul suggests: "Be very careful, then, how you live" (Ephesians 5:15). And, "Live as children of light . . . find out what pleases the Lord" (vv. 8–10). We don't know our "use by" date! So let's make sure we brighten our world with Christ's love today! —JS

DECEMBER 31

The eyes of the LORD your God are continually on [the land] from the beginning of the year to its end. —Deuteronomy 11:12

Longtime California pastor Ray Stedman once told his congregation: "On New Year's Eve we realize more than at any other time in our lives that we can never go back in time. . . . We can look back and remember, but we cannot retrace a single moment of the year that is past." Stedman then referred to the Israelites as they stood on the edge of a new opportunity. After four decades of desert wanderings by their people, this new generation may have wondered if they had the faith and fortitude to possess the Promised Land. Their leader, Moses, reminded them of God's faithfulness (Deuteronomy 11:7) and their destiny (v. 12). Their job was to trust.

On New Year's Eve, we may fear the future because of events in the past. But we need not remain chained to our old memories. We can move ahead focused on God. —DCM

JANUARY 2

*Humans plan their course, but the
LORD establishes their steps.* —Proverbs 16:9

My childhood friend Linda always planned to share God's love by serving as a medical missionary in parts of the world where good care is hard to find. At age 14, Linda began experiencing a chronic health problem that required ongoing hospitalizations—once she spent more than a year in the hospital. Although she has been close to death, Linda remains a most vibrant, grateful, and cheerful person.

Because of her ongoing health issues, her plans worked out in a way far different from how she had hoped. Instead of serving God as a doctor, she serves Him as a patient. No matter how sick she is, the light of the Lord radiates from her. Despite her trials, the genuineness of her faith brings "praise, glory and honor" to Jesus Christ (1 Peter 1:6–7). —JAL

DECEMBER 30

The LORD will go before you, the God of Israel will be your rear guard. —Isaiah 52:12

In late December 1916, a chaplain spoke to British Commonwealth soldiers in Cairo, Egypt. Standing before men whose lives had been turned upside down by World War I, Oswald Chambers talked to them about yesterday and tomorrow. Chambers said, "At the end of the year we turn with eagerness to all that God has for the future . . . God is the God of our yesterdays, and He allows the memory of [our blunders] in order to turn the past into a ministry of spiritual culture for the future. . . . Leave the irreparable past in His hands, and step out into the irresistible future with Him."

God promised Israel He would go before them and protect them (Isaiah 52:12). We can take comfort in knowing that our God will never leave us nor forsake us (Hebrews 13:5). As we end the old year, we can place ourselves—and all our yesterdays and tomorrows—safely in His care. —DCM

JANUARY 3

Hear my prayer, LORD, . . . I dwell with you as a foreigner, a stranger. —Psalm 39:12

When I researched the people in my seminary graduating class recently, I was reminded of life's brevity. Many of them are deceased. Seventy years—give or take a few—and we're gone (Psalm 90:10). David was right: We are strangers here (39:12).

This fleeting nature of our days (39:4) grows more certain as time slips past. The good news is that we dwell with God (39:12), our constant companion, which makes the journey less troubling and less frightening. We may be strangers, but we're never alone (73:23–24). Jesus says, "I am with you always" (Matthew 28:20). We may lose companions who have gone on before, but God never leaves us. And as the saying goes, "Good company on the road makes the way seem lighter." —DHR

DECEMBER 29

There is no one righteous, not even one. —Romans 3:10

A beautiful song to come out of the 1970s was "Bridge Over Troubled Water" by Simon and Garfunkel. That magical melody shows how friendship and selflessness help a person overcome difficult times. I've often thought of the connection between the sacrifice displayed in that tune and the bridge Jesus is for us over the troubled waters of our sin. His death and resurrection create a bridge from this life of trouble to a life of glory and majesty in heaven.

Some of us think of our lives like calm waters. Others face raging waters of trials. However, we all need the bridge Jesus offers. Each of us has sinned (Romans 3:10). Only through God's provision of salvation through Jesus can we take the bridge and enter God's presence. Whether your waters are troubled or untroubled, have you crossed the bridge? —DB

JANUARY 4

I will extol the LORD at all times; his praise will always be on my lips. —Psalm 34:1

While in a Midwestern town on a speaking engagement, I was asked to visit a man who was shut in by poor health. As I entered his little home and saw his situation, I realized that he had no prospect of relief from suffering except through death. Yet listen to what he said to me through his tears: "Brother DeHaan, isn't God good!" Bedfast and deprived of almost everything, this man still had the joy of the Lord. In our short conversation, he attempted to "bless the LORD at all times" (Psalm 34:1 NKJV). There was warmth in his tone as he repeated, "Isn't God good!"

Because our Savior cares for us with immeasurable love, we can determine to trust Him and lean heavily on Him for daily strength. Can we say, no matter how bumpy our path: "Isn't God good!"? —RD

DECEMBER 28

I am making everything new! —Revelation 21:5

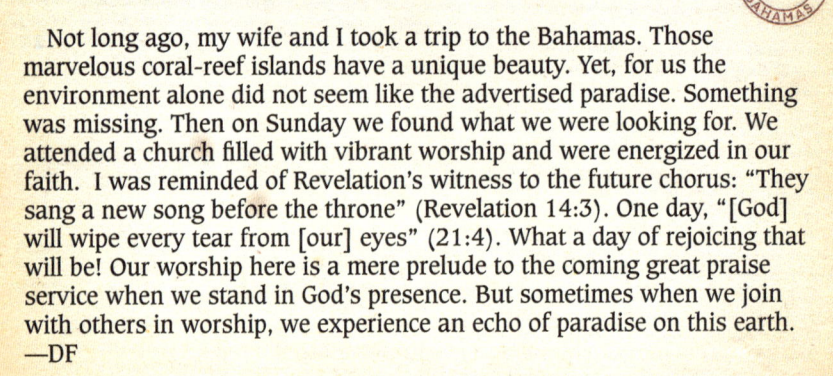

Not long ago, my wife and I took a trip to the Bahamas. Those marvelous coral-reef islands have a unique beauty. Yet, for us the environment alone did not seem like the advertised paradise. Something was missing. Then on Sunday we found what we were looking for. We attended a church filled with vibrant worship and were energized in our faith. I was reminded of Revelation's witness to the future chorus: "They sang a new song before the throne" (Revelation 14:3). One day, "[God] will wipe every tear from [our] eyes" (21:4). What a day of rejoicing that will be! Our worship here is a mere prelude to the coming great praise service when we stand in God's presence. But sometimes when we join with others in worship, we experience an echo of paradise on this earth.
—DF

JANUARY 5

The LORD makes firm the steps of the one who delights in him. —Psalm 37:23

A friend named Al wrote a pamphlet to capture the story of his 86-year-long relationship with our Lord. The key thing I noticed about Al's nearly nine decades of trust was the importance of ordinary choices. He told about memorizing Bible verses, meeting for prayer with others, telling his neighbors about Jesus—all things that changed the direction of his life.

The psalmist wrote, "The LORD makes firm the steps of the one who delights in him" (Psalm 37:23). The passage continues with God's promise of care for all who walk with Him: "Their feet do not slip" (v. 31). Think of God's guidance and faithfulness—the people and experiences that are landmarks on your pathway of faith. Every remembrance of His goodness encourages us to keep traveling with Him in gratefulness. The Lord guides all who walk with Him. —DCM

DECEMBER 27

*I am the Alpha and the Omega, the First and
the Last, the Beginning and the End.* —Revelation 22:13

High atop Mount Corcovado overlooking Rio de Janeiro stands a huge statue of Jesus Christ. The stone monument has stood for nearly sixty years, but now it's beginning to crumble. As Brazilians look for ways to save the statue, we know that even if the statue were to fall, the real Jesus still stands.

It's impossible to honor Jesus adequately by building a statue of Him. He needs no stone memorial. He is alive and is seated today at the right hand of God. And through the indwelling Spirit, He lives in every Christian. Jesus said, "I am the Alpha and the Omega, . . . the Beginning and the End" (Revelation 22:13). He was there before the world began, and He will be here when the world as we know it ends. Jesus is alive and will stand forever! —DB

JANUARY 6

Whatever you have learned or received or heard from me, or seen in me—put it into practice. And the God of peace will be with you. —Philippians 4:9

For nearly an hour I stood by the bed of my dying friend, Francis, the man who had led me to faith in Jesus. I wanted to say something memorable, something meaningful. But for a long time we just exchanged stories—and Francis laughed heartily. Then he got tired, and we got serious. He stopped me before I could say good-bye. He said, "Randy, we've nothing to fear from the story of life because we know how it ends. I'm not afraid. You go do what I've taught you." How like the apostle Paul, who said, "Whatever you have learned or received or heard from me . . . put it into practice" (Philippians 4:9). Francis had no fear.

So much of what I do is touched by Francis. As we journey through life, may we remember those who have encouraged us spiritually. —RK

DECEMBER 26

Whenever you eat this bread and drink this cup, you proclaim the Lord's death until he comes. —1 Corinthians 11:26

Millions of people throng to Jerusalem to look at a tomb some say may have been where Jesus was buried. But no matter what tomb He lay in, Jesus occupied it for only a few days. It has been empty for two thousand years.

Jesus gave us the Lord's Supper (communion) as a memorial to remember Him. On the night He was betrayed, Jesus took bread and the cup and gave thanks to His Father before offering them to His disciples (Luke 22:14–20). Before we partake of those elements, we are to examine ourselves and our relationship with God (1 Corinthians 11:28). "Whenever [we] eat this bread and drink this cup" we are to do so in remembrance of the One we love (vv. 25–26). This enduring memorial reminds us of what He has done for us. —CPH

JANUARY 7

*As a father has compassion on his children,
so the LORD has compassion on those who fear him.* —Psalm 103:13

As I watched a young couple usher their two rambunctious preschoolers on board for our half-hour flight to Grand Rapids, I wondered how they would keep the boys calm for the final journey. When I found my seat, I noticed that the father and one of the sons were behind me. Then I heard the weary father say, "Let's read one of your storybooks." Dad softly and patiently read to his son, keeping him calm.

In one of his psalms David declares, "As a father has compassion on his children, so the LORD has compassion on those who fear him" (Psalm 103:13). This tender word *compassion* shows how deeply our heavenly Father loves His children.

Are you restless in your journey? Snuggle in with God's Book. Your heavenly Father is always near, ready to encourage you with His Word. —BC

DECEMBER 25

The water I give them will become in them a spring of water welling up to eternal life. —John 4:14

In Michigan's Upper Peninsula is a remarkable natural wonder—The Big Spring, a pool fed by underground springs that push more than ten thousand gallons of water a minute through the rocks below and up to the surface. Additionally, the water keeps a constant temperature of forty-five degrees Fahrenheit.

When Jesus encountered a woman at Jacob's well, He told her about a source of water that would always satisfy: "Whoever drinks the water I give them will never thirst. [It] will become in them a spring of water welling up to eternal life" (John 4:14). Far greater than any natural spring is the refreshment we have been offered in Christ himself. We can be satisfied, for Jesus alone, the Water of Life, can quench our thirst. He is the source that never runs dry. —BC

JANUARY 8

My help comes from the LORD,
the Maker of heaven and earth. —Psalm 121:2

As I walk along a favorite trail, I can see a panoramic view of Colorado's Garden of the Gods with majestic Pikes Peak in the background. But from time to time, I walk that section occupied with some problem and find myself looking down at the wide, smooth trail. I remind myself, "David, look up!"

The psalms known as "Songs of Ascents" (Psalm 120–134) were sung by the Israelites as they walked up to Jerusalem to attend pilgrim festivals. Psalm 121 begins, "I lift up my eyes to the mountains—where does my help come from?" (v. 1). The answer follows, "My help comes from the LORD" (v. 2). Along life's path, how we need to keep our eyes fixed on God, our source of help. When we're overwhelmed, it's all right to say aloud, "Look up!" —DCM

DECEMBER 24

When the set time had fully come,
God sent his Son. —Galatians 4:4

How far is it from Nazareth to Bethlehem? If you're in Pennsylvania, it's about nine miles and takes about ten minutes by car. But if you're in Nazareth of Galilee, and you're traveling along with your pregnant wife, as Joseph was, it's about eighty miles and took about a week.

But the journey for the infant Jesus was much farther than eighty miles. He left His place in heaven at God's right hand, came to earth, and accepted our humanity. Eventually, He was stretched out on a cross to die and buried in a borrowed tomb. But the journey was not over. He conquered death, left the tomb, walked again among men, and ascended to heaven. Even that is not the journey's end. Someday He will return as King of kings. Praise God for that first Christmas journey! —DCE

JANUARY 9

My Father's house has many rooms; if that were not so, would I have told you that I am going there to prepare a place for you? —John 14:2

    A thousand strands of time, events, and people weave into a tapestry we call place. Place is where meaning, belonging, and safety come together under the covering of our best efforts at unconditional love. Place beckons us with memories buried deep in our souls. Even when our place isn't perfect, its hold on us is dramatic, magnetic.

    The Bible speaks frequently of place. It's no surprise, then, that Jesus would speak of place when He wants to comfort us. "Do not let your hearts be troubled," He began. Then He added: "I am going there to prepare a place for you" (John 14:1–2). Whatever the struggle, whatever the faltering on your faith journey, remember this: There's a place in heaven already waiting, fitted just for you. Jesus wouldn't have said so if it weren't true. —RK

DECEMBER 23

Your word is a lamp for my feet, a light on my path. —Psalm 119:105

"Now comes the mystery," Henry Ward Beecher (1813–1887) is reputed to have said as his last words. And indeed, few would deny that our departure into the next life is draped in mystery.

The greatest mystery took place when God's Son left his home and stepped into our wonderful, difficult world. In describing the Incarnation, the apostle Paul wrote that Jesus, "being in very nature God, did not consider equality with God something to be used to his own advantage; rather, he made himself nothing by taking the very nature of a servant" (Philippians 2:6–7). Christ saw precisely where he was going; yet He embraced the cross to restore us to His Father. That is the very heart of Christmas.

Because of Christmas, although we walk in mystery we need never walk alone. There is One who longs to go with us. And as we accompany Him, the path always leads home. —TG

JANUARY 10

Let us throw off everything that hinders and the sin that so easily entangles. And let us run with perseverance the race marked out for us. —Hebrews 12:1

August 10, 1628, was a dark day in naval history. On that day the royal warship *Vasa*, which took two years to build, set out on her maiden voyage. Unfortunately, the pride of the Swedish navy sank a mile out to sea. What went wrong? Excess weight pulled the *Vasa* to the bottom of the ocean.

The Christian life can also be weighed down by excess baggage. The writer of Hebrews says: "Let us throw off everything that hinders and the sin that so easily entangles" (12:1). Like the *Vasa*, we may project an impressive exterior. But if we're weighed down with sin, our perseverance will be impaired. By relying on God's guidance and the empowering of the Spirit, our load can be lightened and our perseverance made buoyant. —DF

DECEMBER 22

She gave birth to her firstborn, a son. She wrapped him in cloths and placed him in a manger, because there was no guest room available for them. —Luke 2:7

We had been traveling all day and needed a motel for the night. As we drove, our hopes were dashed time and again by the sight of "No Vacancy" signs. I was frustrated and discouraged. But then I thought of Mary and Joseph in Bethlehem. I imagined Joseph pleading with the manager of the inn, telling him of Mary's condition and their desperate need for a suitable place to give birth. But "there was no guest room available."

Today, two thousand years later, many people still have no room for Jesus. Although they participate in the festivities of the Christmas season, they put up a "No Vacancy" sign. As we celebrate His coming into the world to save sinners, let's make sure there is room in our hearts for Jesus. —RD

JANUARY 11

At the LORD's command they encamped, and at the LORD's command they set out. —Numbers 9:23

I enjoyed watching a corgi named Trevor perform at a dog show. At his master's command, he did a number of complicated activities. After finishing each exercise, he sat down at his master's feet and waited for more instructions. Trevor's careful attention to his master's instruction reminded me of the devotion God desired from His people as they followed Him through the wilderness. "At the LORD's command they encamped, and at the LORD's command they set out" (Numbers 9:23).

God wasn't simply testing the Israelites; He was leading them to the Promised Land—to a better place. So it is with us when God asks us to follow Him. He wants to lead us to a place of closer fellowship with himself. He is loving and faithful in leading those who humbly follow Him. —JBS

DECEMBER 21

My Father's house has many rooms; . . .
I am going there to prepare a place for you. —John 14:2

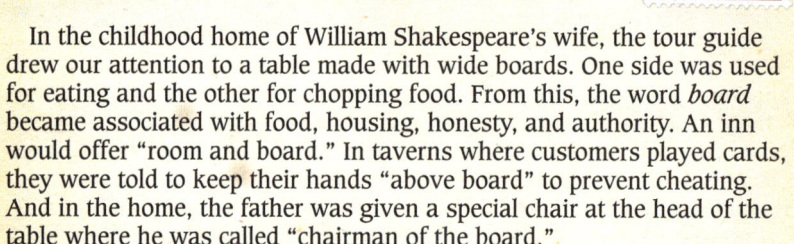

   In the childhood home of William Shakespeare's wife, the tour guide drew our attention to a table made with wide boards. One side was used for eating and the other for chopping food. From this, the word *board* became associated with food, housing, honesty, and authority. An inn would offer "room and board." In taverns where customers played cards, they were told to keep their hands "above board" to prevent cheating. And in the home, the father was given a special chair at the head of the table where he was called "chairman of the board."

   As our "room and board," Jesus is our source of spiritual nourishment (John 6:35, 54), empowers us to live a life of integrity (14:21), is our loving Master (Philippians 2:11), and is even now preparing our eternal home (John 14:2). —DF

JANUARY 12

Praise the LORD, my soul, and forget not all his benefits. —Psalm 103:2

Recently a friend from my youth e-mailed me a picture of our junior high track team. I was instantly swept back in time to happy memories. As I enjoyed the recollections, I also thought of how easily I had forgotten those times.

As we make our way on the journey of life, it's easy to forget important places, people, and events. Time passes, yesterday fades, and we concentrate on current concerns. We can forget how good God has been to us. Perhaps that's why David wrote, "Praise the LORD, my soul, and forget not all his benefits" (Psalm 103:2). Never is this remembrance more needed than when heartaches of life crowd in on us. When we feel overwhelmed, we can recall everything God has done for us. In remembering the past, we find the encouragement to trust Him. —BC

DECEMBER 20

He came as a witness to testify concerning that light, so that through him all might believe. —John 1:7

    The cozy little village of Rjukan, Norway, is located at the foot of a towering mountain and receives no direct sunlight for nearly half the year. Residents had long considered the idea of placing mirrors at the top of the mountain to reflect the sun. Finally, in 2005, "The Mirror Project" began. In October 2013, the mirrors went into action. Residents crowded into the town square to soak up the reflected sunlight.
    In a spiritual sense, much of the world is like this village—mountains of troubles keep the light of Jesus from getting through. And just as sunlight is essential for emotional and physical health, so exposure to the light of Jesus is essential for spiritual health. Thankfully, every believer is in a position to reflect His light into the world's dark places. —JAL

JANUARY 13

Be very careful, then, how you live—not as unwise but as wise. —Ephesians 5:15

One of my favorite places to visit is Dunn's River Falls in Jamaica. Water cascades down a series of rocks as it makes its way to the Caribbean Sea. Adventurers climb the falls, scrambling over rounded rocks on an invigorating trek to the top. The flowing water, the slippery surface, and the steep angles make the going slow and treacherous. To make it safely to the top, climbers must watch every step.

I can't think of a better picture of what Paul is saying in Ephesians 5:15 when he says, "be very careful, then, how you live." With all of life's possible dangers, it's vital that we take each step with Jesus wisely and cautiously. Our goal of following God's example (v.1) is met, Paul says, as we walk carefully in love (vv. 2, 15). —DB

DECEMBER 19

But God demonstrates his own love for us in this:
While we were still sinners, Christ died for us. —Romans 5:8

The giant stone pillars of Stonehenge are a popular tourist attraction and a great source of mystery. Why were they erected? Who accomplished this engineering marvel? The Scriptures speak of a greater mystery—the fact that God came to live among us as a man. Paul wrote in 1 Timothy 3:16, "The mystery from which true godliness springs is great: He appeared in the flesh, was vindicated by the Spirit, was seen by angels, was preached among the nations, was believed on in the world, was taken up in glory."

This brief overview of the life of Christ—the mystery of godliness—is remarkable. What prompted the Creator of the universe, however, is not a mystery. "God demonstrates his own love for us in this: While we were still sinners, Christ died for us" (Romans 5:8). —BC

JANUARY 14

Forgetting what is behind . . . I press on toward the goal to win the prize for which God has called me heavenward in Christ Jesus. —Philippians 3:13–14

Did you know that kangaroos and emus seldom move backward? Kangaroos, because of the shape of their body and the length of their strong tail, cannot shift easily into reverse. And the joints in emus' knees make backward movement difficult. Both animals appear on Australia's coat of arms to symbolize moving forward and making progress.

The apostle Paul called for a similar approach to the life of faith in his letter to the Philippians: "Forgetting what is behind . . . I press on toward the goal to win the prize for which God has called me heavenward in Christ Jesus" (3:13–14). While it's wise to learn from the past, we shouldn't live there. By God's grace we can press forward and serve God faithfully today and in the future. The life of faith is a journey forward. —BC

DECEMBER 18

Let us then approach God's throne of grace with confidence, so that we may receive mercy and find grace to help us in our time of need. —Hebrews 4:16

The beautiful palace of Versailles included an opulent 241-foot-long hall. When a visitor approached the king, he had to curtsy every five steps as he walked the entire distance to meet the king sitting on his silver throne! Foreign emissaries to France submitted to that humiliating ritual to court the French monarch's favor. By contrast, the King of kings invites His people to come to His throne freely and at any time.

Our heavenly Father is much more inviting! "Through [Christ] we . . . have access to the Father by one Spirit" (Ephesians 2:18). Because of this, we can "approach God's throne of grace with confidence" (Hebrew 4:16). Have you responded to God's open invitation? Come in awe and gratitude, for the God of this universe is willing to hear your petitions anytime. —CPH

JANUARY 15

*If anyone is in Christ, the new creation has come:
The old has gone, the new is here!* —2 Corinthians 5:17

Way back in 1933 a nine-year-old boy named Clair prayed to ask Jesus to be his Savior. Clair—my dad—has been on his journey with Christ for eight decades. Growing spiritually is a lifelong process. So how does a new believer feed his faith and continue to grow? Here's what I observed in my dad's life. He read the Scriptures regularly and made prayer a daily part of his life. This helps us grow closer to God and withstand temptation. The Holy Spirit began to develop the "fruit of the Spirit" in him as he surrendered his life in faith and obedience (Galatians 5:22–23).

My dad's spiritual journey continues—and so does ours. What a privilege to have a relationship in which we can "grow in the grace and knowledge of our Lord and Savior Jesus Christ" (2 Peter 3:18). —CHK

DECEMBER 17

The LORD preserves those who are true to him.
—Psalm 31:23

    The castle at Edinburgh, Scotland, was built to provide great security for its citizens. Strategically situated atop a high overlook, its massive walls offered protection for the townspeople whenever invaders approached. Yet as impenetrable as that great fortress seemed, it once fell to hostile forces. This reminds us that man's best efforts never provide complete security against disaster.

    In contrast, David had a perfect protection plan. The Lord was his rock and fortress (Psalm 31:2–3). He trusted in God and was secure amid the attacks of all his foes. Christians are safe in God's strong hands. The psalmist said, "The LORD preserves those who are true to him" (v. 23). We can be certain that He will protect us in death as well as in life! —DCE

JANUARY 16

I have no greater joy than to hear that my children are walking in the truth. —3 John 4

Although he was ill, C. S. Lewis took time to respond to the letter of a child named Philip. After complimenting the boy's fine written expression, Lewis wrote that he was pleased Philip understood that the Narnian lion Aslan represented Jesus Christ. The next day Lewis died, one week before his 65th birthday.

The apostle John, in his later years, sent a letter to his spiritual children. In it we see the joy of a mature believer encouraging his spiritually younger disciples to keep walking in the truth and following Christ. John wrote, "I have no greater joy than to hear that my children are walking in the truth" (3 John 4). Whether by note, e-mail, prayer, or conversation, encouraging spiritual understanding in the next generation should be the pursuit of all mature believers. —DF

DECEMBER 16

I have calmed and quieted myself, I am like a weaned child with its mother. —Psalm 131:2

    The great cathedrals of Europe have intriguing architecture. Because their massive ceilings were too heavy for the walls to support, flying buttresses, or external extensions, were built to support the expansive roofs.

    Although we are "the temple of the living God" (2 Corinthians 6:16), I wonder if we are not more like these cathedrals, with buttresses of external influences like pastors and friends holding us up while we remain weak at the core. Our heart is the place where God meets and relates to us personally. Spending time in His Word and in prayer opens the door for Him to interact with us at the deepest levels of our need and gives Him opportunities to comfort and convict. As we open our hearts to Him, He fans the flame of an intimate, life-changing relationship. —JS

JANUARY 17

Stop and consider God's wonders. —Job 37:14

    Some time ago I drove through the Cascade Mountains in the state of Washington. What breathtaking grandeur! Clear streams of water burst out of rocky crevices high on the mountainside and tumbled down the precipice. Giant trees felled by lightning or broken by avalanches of snow lay silent in the ravines below. Then, as I descended from the mountain pass, a beautiful valley spread before me with its rich orchards, and beyond was a green plateau covered with a new crop of wheat. A swift-flowing river ran parallel to the highway. As I drove through this beauty, I found myself talking out loud as praise to God leaped from my heart.

    Take time today to observe the marvels of creation that surround you. Your soul will be thrilled as you "stop and consider God's wonders."
—PVG

DECEMBER 15

Moses cried out to the LORD, and the LORD showed him a piece of wood. —Exodus 15:25

Robyn and Steve have a ministry that provides little income. Recently, a family crisis forced them to embark on a five-thousand-mile round trip in their well-used minivan. About two thousand miles from home, their van began to sputter and stall. The diagnosis: "You need a new engine." Unable to afford one, they had no choice but to coax the van home. Three days, a case of oil, and many prayers later, they miraculously limped into their driveway. Then they heard of a "car missionary" who assisted people in ministry. He replaced the engine free of charge. If Steve had gotten the van fixed en route, it would have cost thousands of dollars.

Even when our situation looks difficult, we can trust that God is leading. He already knows what we'll need when we get there. —DB

JANUARY 18

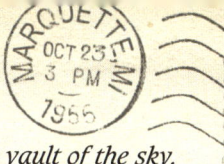

Let birds fly above the earth across the vault of the sky.
—Genesis 1:20

When my dog Whitaker and I take our morning walk through the deep woods of Michigan's Upper Peninsula, the air is filled with sound. Birds of many species break the early morning silence with their songs. "Isn't God great!" I say to Whit. I thank God for the wonderful variety of sounds with which He fills His woods. He created hundreds of varieties of birds, each with its own color and habits and call. "And God saw that it was good" (Genesis 1:20–21).

As I continue my walk with Whitaker, my heart is filled with thankfulness to God for the multitude of sights and sounds and species that enrich our world. I praise Him for His creativity in not only forming our world but for making it so beautiful—and good. —DCE

DECEMBER 14

*[God will] provide a way out so that
[we] can endure it.* —1 Corinthians 10:13

    Highway 77, which passes through the Appalachian Mountains in West Virginia, features a series of runaway truck ramps. These semi-paved exits appear in an area of the highway where the altitude drops nearly thirteen hundred feet over the course of about six miles. This steep descent combined with the road's winding path can create problems for motorists—especially truck drivers.
    Just as a runaway truck needs an escape route from a highway, we also need "a way of escape" when out-of-control desires threaten our spiritual well-being. When we face temptation, "[God will] provide a way out so that [we] can endure it" (1 Corinthians 10:13). He enables us to say "no" to enticement through the power of His Word. God is faithful. He will provide a way for us to resist sin's allure. —JBS

JANUARY 19

I will put in the desert the cedar and the acacia, the myrtle and the olive. I will set junipers in the wasteland, the fir and the cypress together. —Isaiah 41:19

On the Canadian side of the majestic Niagara Falls is a greenhouse with a vast array of beautiful flowers and exotic plants. It contains a plaque that reads: "Enter, friends, and view God's pleasant handiwork, the embroidery of earth." The "embroidery of earth" includes the verdant rainforests of Brazil, the frigid beauty of Arctic Circle glaciers, and the sweeping reaches of the fertile Serengeti in Africa. These areas, like those described in Isaiah 41, remind us to praise God for His creative handiwork.

The wonder of individual plants is also part of God's work. From the crocus (Isaiah 35:1) to the myrtle, cypress, and cedar (Isaiah 41:19–20), God colors our world with a splendorous display of beauty. Enjoy the wonder. —DB

DECEMBER 13

I planted the seed, Apollos watered it, but God has been making it grow. —1 Corinthians 3:6

The English explorer Captain Cook is said to have taken seeds from his native land on his many voyages. Every time he set foot on foreign soil, he would quietly scatter them wherever he thought they would thrive. Thus in faraway places where no British subjects dwelt, flowers and herbs of England began to flourish.

God intends that the truth of His Word should fall on the good ground of receptive hearts and spring up and grow. Jesus sowed through preaching and teaching, and every Christian is charged with the work of continuing to spread the good news wherever they are. Our responsibility is to be faithful in our witness for Christ and to believe that the Lord will give the increase. Are you sowing the seed of the gospel as you journey through this world? —PVG

JANUARY 20

You are a forgiving God, gracious and compassionate. —Nehemiah 9:17

Fifteen years after trusting Jesus at age ten, Jim's commitment had faded. He adopted a live-for-the-moment philosophy and developed some bad habits. Then his life seemed to fall apart. Fears and doubts plagued Jim. Nothing seemed to help—until he read Psalm 121:2, "My help comes from the LORD, the Maker of heaven and earth." These words cut through the fear and confusion in his heart. He turned back to God, and God welcomed him.

Sounds like ancient Israel, doesn't it? The Israelites spent many years rebelling and ignoring God's goodness, turning away to follow their own path (Nehemiah 9:16–21). Yet when they repented, God was "ready to pardon, gracious and merciful" (v. 17 NKJV). Have you wandered away a bit? Draw near to God again. He will show compassion and welcome you back to closeness with Him. —JBS

DECEMBER 12

Always learning but never able to come to a knowledge of the truth. —2 Timothy 3:7

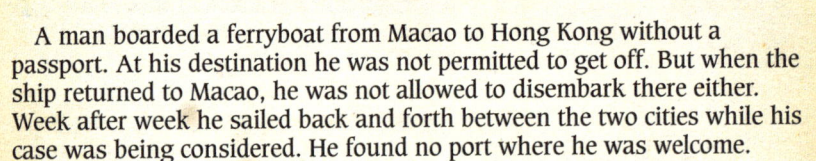

    A man boarded a ferryboat from Macao to Hong Kong without a passport. At his destination he was not permitted to get off. But when the ship returned to Macao, he was not allowed to disembark there either. Week after week he sailed back and forth between the two cities while his case was being considered. He found no port where he was welcome.

    Some people can be like that. They shuttle from one religious philosophy to another, looking for some assurance about their eternal destiny. But spiritually they never find a harbor where they can anchor their souls. You don't need to be without a country. By faith you can accept God's gracious provision in Christ, who alone offers a passport to heaven. Your weary soul will find a welcome in the Savior. —PVG

JANUARY 21

He will not let your foot slip—he who watches over you will not slumber. —Psalm 121:3

In his book *A Sweet and Bitter Providence*, John Piper offers these notes: "Life is not a straight line leading from one blessing to the next and then finally to heaven. Life is a winding and troubled road. . . . [God] is plotting the course and managing the troubles with far-reaching purposes for our good and for the glory of Jesus Christ."

The Jews journeying to Jerusalem for the annual feasts (Deuteronomy 16:16) had the assurance of knowing that God was plotting their course and managing the troubled roads for them. They expressed this assurance in Psalm 121, a pilgrim song. The Lord, who rescued Israel, would continue to help, preserve, and walk with His people.

Life is a winding road with unknown perils and troubles, but we can be certain of God's providence, security, and care. —MW

DECEMBER 11

People are destined to die once, and after that to face judgment. —Hebrews 9:27

In Valladolid, Spain, where Christopher Columbus died, stands a monument commemorating the great discoverer. It features a statue of a lion destroying one of the Latin words that had been part of Spain's motto for centuries. Before Columbus made his voyages, the Spaniards thought they had reached the outer limits of earth. Thus their motto was "Ne Plus Ultra," which means "No More Beyond." The word being torn away by the lion is "Ne" or "no," making it read "Plus Ultra." Columbus had proven that there was indeed "more beyond."

The words "Plus Ultra" also apply to what lies beyond the grave. What we do with Christ and His offer of salvation settles for us whether our "more beyond" will be filled with everlasting joy or endless regret. —PVG

JANUARY 22

Precious in the sight of the LORD is the death of his faithful servants. —Psalm 116:15

On March 1, 1981, preacher and Bible scholar D. Martyn Lloyd-Jones lay on his deathbed. Indicating that he did not want any more prayers for his recovery, he wrote on a piece of paper: "Do not hold me back from glory."

Because life is precious, it can be hard to let our loved ones go. Yet Psalm 116:15 tells us, "Precious in the sight of the LORD is the death of his faithful servants." When Paul saw that death was near, he was encouraged by what awaited him in heaven: "There is in store for me the crown of righteousness" (2 Timothy 4:8).

As Christians, our ultimate destination is to "be with Christ, which is better by far" (Philippians 1:23). This should give us confidence in facing life's challenges and comfort when other believers leave us for heaven. —DF

DECEMBER 10

He stilled the storm to a whisper; the waves of the sea were hushed. They were glad when it grew calm, and he guided them to their desired haven. —Psalm 107:29–30

The poet Alfred, Lord Tennyson was being taken to his winter residence. As the boat crossed the strait, Tennyson heard a moaning sound as the waves dashed against a large sandbar. He knew a storm was coming but that it would not prevent his crossing. A few days later, Tennyson's health began to fail. His nurse urged him to write a hymn to "help and comfort other sufferers." The next morning he handed her a scrap of paper. The poem was filled with imagery about the sea and the emotions related to dying, which the "moaning of the bar" had brought to his mind, and expressed the glorious hope of seeing Jesus at the end of life's voyage. Dying may seem ominous, but those who love Jesus will be piloted safely to the "desired haven"! —HGB

JANUARY 23

[God] will wipe every tear from their eyes. There will be no more death or mourning or crying. —Revelation 21:4

A tragic event in US history was the forced relocation of Native Americans. In the winter of 1838, thousands of Cherokee were forced to embark on a brutal 1,000-mile march westward known as The Trail of Tears. This injustice resulted in the deaths of thousands of people.

Injustice, pain, and heartache are still part of life today. Many people feel as if they are leaving a trail of tears—unnoticed tears and uncomforted grief. But our Lord sees our tears and comforts our weary hearts (2 Corinthians 1:3–5). He reminds us of a day when "God will wipe every tear. . . . There will be no more death or mourning or crying" (Revelation 21:4). The God who offers freedom from tears in the future is the only One who can fully comfort our tears now. —BC

DECEMBER 9

Then they were willing to take him into the boat, and immediately the boat reached the shore where they were heading. —John 6:21

The poem "Invictus" says in part, "I am the master of my fate: I am the captain of my soul." This message is dangerous. A young captain was approaching land when a passenger familiar with maritime procedures asked if he intended to anchor the ship and call for help in entering the harbor. "Anchor? Not I! I expect to be in dock with the morning tide." The passenger persisted, urging him to signal for a pilot. "I am my own pilot," he replied. Determined to reach port by morning, he took a narrow channel to shorten the distance. His vessel was wrecked, and his own life was lost.

Our voyage through time and into eternity is too treacherous to attempt without God's help. Let's seek His guidance to make it safely to the heavenly shore. —PVG

JANUARY 24

Do not be surprised at the fiery ordeal that has come on you to test you, . . . but rejoice . . . when his glory is revealed. —1 Peter 4:12–13

You can learn a lot by walking with others through tough times. That was the case for us as our friends Sam and Carol trudged through Sam's cancer journey. For a year we watched and prayed as he endured the treatment and the pain. And just when it seemed he was in the clear, the cancer roared back. The disappointment was obvious. Year two looked a lot like year one as Sam went through chemo, sickness, and side effects all over again. But when Sam told us about his tough road ahead, he said: "We want to make sure that through it all God gets the glory." Sam was anticipating the time when God's "glory is revealed" (1 Peter 4:13).

What mountains do you face? Like Sam and Carol, you too can depend on God's grace. —DB

DECEMBER 8

This terrified them and they asked, "What have you done?" (They knew he was running away from the LORD, because he had already told them so.) —Jonah 1:10

In 1748 John Newton, a seaman who had turned his back on God, was aboard a trading ship headed for England. Suddenly a fierce Atlantic wind rudely awakened him. As with Jonah, his vessel nearly broke apart. While the damaged ship drifted at sea, Newton prayed for God's mercy and put his faith in Jesus. That's how a blasphemous, disreputable seaman became, by God's grace, the godly penman of the words of the beloved hymn "Amazing Grace."

If you, like Jonah, are a child of God who has strayed or who has deliberately run away from the Lord, come home. Live for Him again. Or maybe you're like John Newton. You need to trust Jesus for salvation. Don't wait for one of life's storms to awaken you to your need. Turn to Christ today. —DB

JANUARY 25

They were longing for a better country—
a heavenly one. —Hebrews 11:16

We wondered why a friend kept traveling to Hobart, Tasmania. When she invited us to join her there, we journeyed for a long time, sometimes enduring hairpin turns and humdrum travel as we went from the airport to her place. Nothing extraordinary. But as we drove up a steep driveway, the spectacular panorama of the city and the bay became clear. Suddenly we knew why she made the trip.

The lives of the pioneers of faith in Hebrews 11 had their share of "hairpin turns" and "humdrum" situations. But they pressed on. Why? Their destination was "the city with foundations, whose architect and builder is God" (v.10). Today, whether life is ordinary or difficult, keep pressing on. At the end of the journey, you will see the amazing place God has prepared for us! —CPH

DECEMBER 7

Therefore I tell you, whatever you ask for in prayer, believe that you have received it, and it will be yours.
—Mark 11:24

When missionary Hudson Taylor went to China, he traveled by sailing ship. One day, the captain came to his door. "Mr. Taylor," he said, "we have no wind. We are drifting toward an island where . . . I fear they are cannibals." "What can I do?" asked Taylor. The captain replied, "I understand that you believe in God. I want you to pray for wind." "All right, Captain," said Taylor, "I will, but you must set the sail." The captain argued but finally agreed. Forty-five minutes later he returned and found the missionary still on his knees. "You can stop praying now," said the captain. "We've got more wind than we know what to do with!"

Hudson Taylor believed that God answers prayer. What about you? Do you really expect Him to respond? Pray and then "set the sail." —PVG

JANUARY 26

*When my spirit grows faint within me,
it is you who watch over my way.*
—Psalm 142:3

Are you overwhelmed with sadness today? It may be the weight of a difficult ministry; the worry of a hard marriage; the sorrow of a struggling child. "Surely," you say, "God would not have me walk this way. There must be an easier path." But are any of us wise enough to know that some other way would make us better and wiser? No, our Father in heaven knows the best path to bring us to completion (Psalm 142:3).

His ways are higher than our ways; His thoughts are higher than our thoughts (Isaiah 55:9). We can humbly take the path He has marked out for us and do so in absolute trust in His infinite wisdom and love. He will not lead us astray. —DHR

DECEMBER 6

But he said to them, "It is I; don't be afraid."
—John 6:20

    Thomas Kelly told about his first voyage down the St. Lawrence River. The Long Sault Rapids came into view with their rushing, foaming waters. While still a safe distance away, the boat was anchored and a new pilot was taken on board. The pilot steered the boat toward the center of the rapids. With eyes riveted on an object beyond the torrent, he held the vessel steady as it moved through the rushing current and protruding rocks. He knew precisely what he was doing, and soon the danger was behind them.
    Life is like the perilous waters of those rapids. The only way to navigate through them is to receive Jesus as your personal Savior, trust Him as the pilot of your life, and let Him take complete control. With Christ in command, you'll make it safely through. —PVG

JANUARY 27

This happened that we might not rely on ourselves but on God, who raises the dead. —2 Corinthians 1:9

In August 2009, Blair and Ronna Martin lost their energetic nine-year-old son Matti in a tragic accident. An observation made by Matti's mom is valuable for anyone walking through the valley. Ronna was reading 2 Corinthians 1:9, which says that "we might not rely on ourselves but on God, who raises the dead." She felt as if Jesus were telling her, "Ronna, I know the journey has been too much for you. Do not be ashamed of your exhaustion. Instead, see it as an opportunity for Me to take charge of your life."

When the journey gets too tough to navigate, remember that we don't travel alone. "My strength and my hope have to be in Christ alone," Ronna said. That's a truth we all need as we travel the journey God has for us. —DB

DECEMBER 5

All things are wearisome, more than one can say. The eye never has enough of seeing, nor the ear its fill of hearing. —Ecclesiastes 1:8

Our world has many things that appeal to us. Apart from what is sinful, we can and should enjoy its pleasures. A delicious meal graced with the good fellowship of friends warms our hearts. The beauties of nature inspire and fill us with wonder. Good music refreshes our souls. And work itself can be fulfilling.

Yes, even in a sin-cursed world we can find great enjoyment. And yet these pursuits do not bring full and lasting satisfaction. If we live only for self-gratification, no matter how lofty our achievements, we long for more. It makes no difference how deeply we drink of the wells of this world's pleasures—our thirst is never satisfied. "All of it is meaningless, a chasing after the wind" (Ecclesiastes 2:17). Only in the Christ-filled life do we experience true satisfaction. —RD

JANUARY 28

As Jesus was walking beside the Sea of Galilee, he saw two brothers, Simon called Peter and his brother Andrew. "Come, follow me," Jesus said. —Matthew 4:18–19

I love to walk Idaho's picturesque paths and trails. I'm often reminded that these treks are symbolic of our spiritual journey as we walk with Jesus as our companion. He walked through the land of Israel, gathering disciples, saying to them, "Follow Me" (Matthew 4:19).

Only God knows where our path will take us, but we have our Lord's assurance, "I am with you always" (Matthew 28:20). There is not one hour without His presence, not one mile without His companionship. That makes the journey lighter. —DHR

DECEMBER 4

In God I trust and am not afraid. What can mere mortals do to me? —Psalm 56:4

Huge waves washed into the little boat, threatening to sink it. Terrified, Jesus' disciples woke Him. How could He sleep through the shrieking winds? "Teacher, don't you care if we drown?" they shouted (Mark 4:38). Calmly Jesus arose and commanded the raging storm to cease. Then, amid the calm and the darkness, He asked His disciples: "Why are you so afraid? Do you still have no faith?" (v. 40).

As we voyage through the sea of life, illness and loss may threaten to overwhelm us. In our anxiety we may cry out to our seemingly indifferent Lord, "Don't you care about our problems?" And Christ, completely in control of every circumstance, gently rebukes us and urges us to trust His almighty and all-wise sovereignty. When God is with us, we are safe for time and eternity. —VG

JANUARY 29

His name alone is exalted; his splendor is above the earth and the heavens. —Psalm 148:13

You don't have to snorkel the warm waters of Jamaica to be impressed with the hidden beauty of our planet's seas, but it helps. You don't have to view the Rockies or gaze at Mount Fuji to realize how awe-inspiring are the vistas of our globe, but it helps.

Experiencing firsthand the majesty of the mountains and the glory of the oceans can leave us breathless as we ponder how spectacular the earth really is. But celebrating the greatness of our unique planet should remind us that we are merely "the people of his pasture" (Psalm 95:7). The creation was flung into space to point to God's greatness, power, and majesty. He alone deserves our praise (Psalm 148:5). —DB

DECEMBER 3

Direct my footsteps according to your word.
—Psalm 119:133

During the era of great sea exploration in the fifteenth and sixteenth centuries, sailing ships traversed vast, hazardous oceans and navigated dangerous coastlines. Pilots used various navigation techniques—including a book called a "rutter," a log of events kept by earlier voyagers who chronicled their encounters with previously unknown and difficult waters. By reading the sailing details in a rutter, captains could avoid hazards and make it through difficult waters.

In many ways, the Christian life is like a voyage, and the believer needs help in navigating life's perilous seas. We have that help because God has given us His Word as a "spiritual rutter." As you reflect on the teaching in the Bible, you'll be reminded of God's past care, assured of the Lord's guidance in trying circumstances, and warned against sinfulness. —DF

JANUARY 30

All Scripture is God-breathed and is useful for teaching, rebuking, correcting and training in righteousness. —2 Timothy 3:16

Whenever you take a route with the help of your GPS, you can expect at least once to hear that voice saying, "Recalculating." It's reassuring to know that it's getting ready to get you back on the right road.

Did you ever think of the Bible as life's spiritual navigation system? "All Scripture is God-breathed and is useful for teaching, rebuking, correcting and training in righteousness" (2 Timothy 3:16). Doctrine tells us which road to travel; reproof tells us when we're off the road; correction tells us how to get back on; instruction in righteousness tells us how to stay on God's road. The moment we veer off course, the Holy Spirit is "recalculating" and urging us to return to the Father's way. Let's listen closely to the Spirit's directions. —DCM

DECEMBER 2

The word of the LORD is right and true; he is faithful in all he does. —Psalm 33:4

The unspoken code among the settlers of the American West was that a man always kept his word. That explains why Andrew Garcia made a 1,300-mile trek in 1879 to pay a debt. In the previous year he had borrowed money to pay for supplies in Bozeman, Montana. He promised to pay back the loan by January 1. The winter snows came early, however, and Garcia couldn't get back. Finally, a year later, he traveled from New Mexico to Bozeman to pay back his debt. Garcia believed in keeping his word.

Followers of Christ should also be known as people of integrity. God never breaks His promises (Psalm 33:4). Like Him, let's be true to our word. —HVL

JANUARY 31

The LORD your God led you all the way in the wilderness these forty years, to humble and test you in order to know what was in your heart. —Deuteronomy 8:2

Whenever I read the books of Moses, I wonder how many times he heard "Are we there yet?" from the Israelites. Moses had told his people that God would lead them to "a land flowing with milk and honey" (Exodus 3:8). He did, but first they spent forty years wandering in the wilderness. After four hundred years of slavery, the Hebrews needed to have their hearts, souls, and minds reoriented toward God. This was accomplished in the wilderness (Deuteronomy 8:2, 15–18), but not before an entire generation died because of disobedience (Numbers 32:13).

In life, sometimes we want to ask God, "Are we there yet?" It helps to remember that the journey, not just the destination, is important to God. He uses it to humble us, test us, and show us what is in our hearts. —JAL

DECEMBER 1

Rejoice with me; I have found my lost sheep. —Luke 15:6

In my college years I worked as a guide, taking boys on treks into Rocky Mountain National Park in Colorado. On one occasion one of my hikers lagged behind and took the wrong fork on a trail. When we arrived at our campsite he was nowhere to be found. I frantically went out to search for him. Just before dark, I came across him sitting by a small lake—lost and alone. In my joy, I gave him a bear hug, hoisted him on my shoulders, and carried him down the trail to his companions.

Jesus, the Son of Man, "came to seek and to save the lost" (Luke 19:10). No matter how far you may have strayed and how lost you may be, He came to seek and to save you. —DHR

FEBRUARY 1

For you make me glad by your deeds, LORD; I sing for joy at what your hands have done. —Psalm 92:4

    I've always thought that you can see the hand of God best in the rearview mirror. In my own life, I get a lot of clarity about the wise ways of God as I reflect on how He has managed my journey by "what [his] hands have done" (Psalm 92:4). Looking ahead, though, is not always so clear. Have you ever had that lost feeling when the road ahead seems twisted, foggy, and scary? Before you move ahead, stop and look in the rearview mirror, and joyfully realize that God meant it when He said, " 'Never will I leave you; never will I forsake you.' So we say with confidence, 'The Lord is my helper; I will not be afraid' " (Hebrews 13:5–6).

    With the promise of God's presence and help in mind, you can move ahead with utmost confidence. —JS

NOVEMBER 30

But very truly I tell you, it is for your good that I am going away. Unless I go away, the Advocate will not come to you; but if I go, I will send him to you. —John 16:7

After living for two years in the far North, an Arctic explorer wrote a brief message on a piece of paper, inserted it into a small capsule, and tied it to a carrier pigeon's body. He flung the pigeon from his ship out into the icy cold weather. The bird flew two thousand miles over ice and ocean to Norway, dropping at last into the lap of the explorer's wife. Her joy was inexpressible: Her husband was alive!

Even as the explorer's wife knew he was alive because of the message brought to her by the pigeon, so we who are saved are assured that Christ is living because of the Holy Spirit He sent to indwell us. What joy floods our soul as He testifies about the Lord Jesus through His precious Word (John 16:13–14). —HGB

FEBRUARY 2

They devoted themselves to the apostles' teaching. —Acts 2:42

One sunny day when my neighbor responded to my "Hello" with a negative, "It's just another Sunday," I wasn't sure what he meant. Was he saying, "I'm just going through the motions of another day"?

We can do that with church attendance: "It's just another Sunday." In the early church (Acts 2:41–47), everyone was a new believer—so they were bound to be enthusiastic. But what about us? How can we make each Sunday special? Go anticipating meeting with God. God is with us in a unique way as we gather with others who know Him (Matthew 18:20; James 4:8). Go to learn about God. We can always be encouraged by God's Word (Psalm 119:105). Expect to hear from Him. Go to fellowship with others. We need each other!

Lord, help it not be just another Sunday. —AC

NOVEMBER 29

The woman had taken the two men and hidden them. —Joshua 2:4

In 1803 Lewis and Clark led an expedition across an unexplored America to the Pacific coast. Along the way a French fur trader and his wife, Sacajawea, joined them. Sacajawea served as interpreter and guide. During the trip, Sacajawea was reunited with her older brother who helped them acquire horses and a map of the uncharted West. Without Sacajawea's and her brother's help, the expedition may not have succeeded.

The Bible tells of another expedition that received unexpected help. The Israelites had sent spies into Jericho. There, Rahab agreed to ensure their escape in exchange for her family's protection. In this way God used her to prepare the way for a victory in Israel's conquest of the Promised Land.

Are you in the middle of a challenge? Remember, God can provide help from unexpected sources. —DF

FEBRUARY 3

You, God, are my God, earnestly I seek you; I thirst for you, my whole being longs for you, in a dry and parched land where there is no water. —Psalm 63:1

As followers of Christ, we want to draw closer to Jesus. But along the way, we're distracted and succumb to the pull of alluring, lesser things. When that happens, we cease our pursuit of Jesus and begin to gravitate toward stuff that is empty and unsatisfying.

Psalm 63 is the cure for lives being pulled the wrong direction. David pursued God, knowing that He alone could satisfy his inner longings because His "love is better than life" (v. 3). The joy of God's presence consumed every moment: "On my bed I remember you; I think of you through the watches of the night" (v. 6). David understood that true joy and purpose come from chasing hard after God. Let's get back on track and pursue an increasingly closer walk with God! —JS

NOVEMBER 28

We are co-workers in God's service.
—1 Corinthians 3:9

On May 29, 1953, New Zealander Edmund Hillary and his guide Tenzing Norgay became the first people to reach the peak of Mount Everest. Later, journalists repeatedly asked who had reached the summit first. The expedition leader replied, "They reached it together, as a team."

It's counterproductive to try to determine who deserves the most credit when something is done well. The church at Corinth was divided between those who followed Paul and those who followed Apollos. Paul told them, "I planted the seed, Apollos watered it" (1 Corinthians 3:6). He reminded them that they were "co-workers in God's service" (v. 9) and that God gave the increase in ministry (v. 7). Our concern about who deserves the credit serves only to take away the honor and glory that belong to Jesus alone. —CPH

FEBRUARY 4

You turned to God from idols to serve the living and true God. —1 Thessalonians 1:9

When Paul addressed the people in Athens, he was grieved by the idolatry in that city. Yet he used the people's imperfect understanding of God to point them to the God of Scripture. Of their efforts in trying to find God, Paul said: "The God who made the world and everything in it is the Lord of heaven and earth and does not live in temples built by human hands" (Acts 17:24).

In our increasingly pluralistic world, the people around us may worship a multiplicity of deities. Yet their spiritual journey need not end there. We never know when someone might be moving toward the kingdom of God. Following the example of Paul, we should respect a person's religious background, watch for spiritual receptivity, and then point him or her to the one true God of Scripture. —DF

NOVEMBER 27

The LORD reigns, he is robed in majesty;
the LORD is robed in majesty and armed with strength. —Psalm 93:1

Iguazu Falls on the border of Brazil and Argentina is a spectacular waterfall system of 275 falls along 2.7 km (1.67 miles) of the Iguazu River. Etched on a wall on the Brazilian side of the falls are the words of Psalm 93:4, "Mightier than the thunders of many waters, mightier than the waves of the sea, the LORD on high is mighty!" (RSV). Below it are these words, "God is always greater than all of our troubles."

The writer of Psalm 93, who penned its words during a time when kings reigned, knew that God is the ultimate King over all. "The LORD reigns," he wrote. "Your throne was established long ago; you are from all eternity" (vv. 1–2). No matter how high the floods or waves, the Lord remains greater than them all. —CPH

FEBRUARY 5

Enoch walked faithfully with God; then he was no more, because God took him away. —Genesis 5:24

Years after Charlie Duke spent three days on the moon with the Apollo 16 program, he had a spiritual transformation. It began when his friend invited him to a Bible study, and Charlie prayed to trust Christ. He experienced an indescribable peace that was so profound he began to share his story with others. Charlie told them, "My walk on the moon lasted three days, and it was a great adventure. But my walk with God lasts forever."

The Bible tells of another man who walked with God. "Enoch walked faithfully with God; then he was no more, because God took him away" (Genesis 5:24). God took him directly into eternity (see Hebrews 11:5). We can learn a lesson from Charlie and Enoch. For believers, no matter where our journey leads, our walk with God will last for eternity! —DF

NOVEMBER 26

He gives strength to the weary and increases the power of the weak. —Isaiah 40:29

When I was a teenager, my dad and I enjoyed many fishing trips together. But one trip was nearly a disaster. We drove up into a high mountain range and set up camp in a remote area. After a long day of fishing, it was time to return to camp. But as we walked, Dad grew pale and nauseated and had little strength. I had him sit down and drink water. Then I prayed aloud to God for help. Bolstered by prayer, rest, and nourishment, Dad improved, and I slowly led him back to camp.

Do you feel like you have little strength to go on? If so, recall God's promise: "He gives strength to the weary" (Isaiah 40:29). Ask God for help, and depend on Him for strength to continue. —DF

FEBRUARY 6

We are surrounded by such a great cloud of witnesses.
—Hebrews 12:1

Along the old Oregon Trail in Idaho is a giant lava boulder known as Register Rock. It's located at a favorite overnight camping area for westbound immigrants in the nineteenth century. Travelers often inscribed their names on the rock, so Register Rock stands as a monument to their courage and tenacity.

When I think of Register Rock, I think of other pilgrims. Hebrews 11 lists some: Gideon, Barak, Samson, Jephthah, David, and Samuel, to name a few. But there are other more recent pilgrims: my mother and father, my fifth-grade Sunday school teacher, my youth leader, my mentors Ray Stedman and Howard Hendricks, and a host of others. Their names are written in my memory. We should remember the "pilgrims" who have gone before us. As a tribute to them, let's follow their faith. —DHR

NOVEMBER 25

Give thanks to the LORD for his unfailing love and his wonderful deeds for mankind. —Psalm 107:8

William Bradford sat down at the first Thanksgiving meal in 1621 after starvation and sickness had wiped out over half of the members of the Massachusetts settlement the previous winter. Despite this loss, a spirit of gratefulness surged within Bradford. His journal entry about the feast echoed Psalm 107: "[they] were ready to perish in this wilderness but they cried unto the Lord, and He heard their voice, and looked on their adversity. Let them therefore praise the Lord, because He is good, and His mercies endure forever."

Bradford and the other colonists were thankful to be alive, seeing themselves as proof of God's mercy. We can be grateful to God for our lives as well. His goodness is obvious when we're safe and content, but it also sustains us through desperate days. —JBS

FEBRUARY 7

Now I want you to know, brothers and sisters, that what has happened to me has actually served to advance the gospel. —Philippians 1:12

On the apostle Paul's fourth missionary journey, he was traveling as a prisoner, bound for trial before Caesar in Rome. We might be tempted to call this an unfortunate time in Paul's life, if it were not for his view that God was leading and using him just as much on this journey as He did on the previous three. He wrote: "what has happened to me has actually served to advance the gospel" and "it has become clear throughout the whole palace guard and to everyone else that I am in chains for Christ" (Philippians 1:12–13).

Even when our journey in life is marked by confinement and limitations, we can be sure that the Lord will encourage others through us as we speak His Word and trust in Him. —DCM

NOVEMBER 24

You suffered along with those in prison and joyfully accepted the confiscation of your property, because you knew that you yourselves had better and lasting possessions. —Hebrews 10:34

In Genesis we read of the great famine in ancient Egypt. Tradition says that when Joseph opened his storehouses filled with grain, he gave orders for the chaff to be thrown into the Nile. By letting it float downriver to the suffering people who lived below, he was telling them there was abundant provision reserved for them farther up the stream.

The spiritual blessings that come to us by way of divine grace are almost like husks compared to the good things prepared for us in the wonderful life beyond. Faith and love may glow warmly in our hearts now. Yet this joy is only a preview of the glory that awaits us. If the blessings of salvation thrill us now, what will we experience when God shows us "the incomparable riches of his grace"? (Ephesians 2:7). —HGB

FEBRUARY 8

You guide me with your counsel, and afterward you will take me into glory. —Psalm 73:24

One of my favorite boyhood pastimes was walking the creek behind our home. If I made it to the creek mouth, my dog and I would sit and share lunch by the lake. We'd linger as long as we could, but my father wanted me home before sunset. Our house sat on a hill behind some trees, but the light was always on until I got home. Dad would be on the back porch, waiting. "How did it go?" he'd ask. "Pretty good," I'd say. "But it sure is good to be home."

My life's journey is a bit like that. I know at the end there's a caring Father and my eternal home. I can hardly wait! My heavenly Father is waiting for me. I suppose He'll ask, "How did it go?" "Pretty good," I'll say. "But it's sure good to be home." —DHR

NOVEMBER 23

[God] has blessed us . . . with every spiritual blessing in Christ. —Ephesians 1:3

   In Siena, Tuscany, a delicatessen's storefront window displays a mouthwatering assortment of cured meats, artisan cheeses, and baskets of bread. So many specialty food products make the store delightfully overwhelming. Similarly, the Bible reminds us of the abundance we have through Jesus. God has given believers "every spiritual blessing in Christ" (Ephesians 1:3). Through Jesus, we have God's unconditional love, forgiveness for sin, and promise of eternal life. We have peace, wisdom, and more. It's not uncommon for this bounty to spill over and bless others. For example, when we're offended, we forgive because God forgives us. Or, if we sense someone is hurting, we extend love because God has lavished His love on us. Like a storefront window packed with tantalizing treats, our lives can advertise the bounty of God's spiritual blessings. —JBS

FEBRUARY 9

While they were worshiping the Lord and fasting, the Holy Spirit said, "Set apart for me Barnabas and Saul for the work to which I have called them." —Acts 13:2

Three months before an overseas missions trip, a friend and I were talking about it. He said, "If anyone can't go, I'd be willing to step in." A few weeks later, there was an opening, so I e-mailed him to see if he was still interested. "Sure," he responded. "I got a passport just in case." He was ready. My friend's preparation reminds me of a first-century story. Paul and Barnabas were getting ready for whatever God might ask them to do or wherever He might send them. They prepared by "worshiping the Lord and fasting" (Acts 13:2). When the Holy Spirit said, "Set apart for me Barnabas and Saul for the work" (v. 2), they were all set. Are you preparing for what the Spirit might want you to do? When He says, "Go," will you be ready? —DB

NOVEMBER 22

I know what it is to be in need, and I know what it is to have plenty. I have learned the secret of being content in any and every situation, whether well fed or hungry, whether living in plenty or in want.
—Philippians 4:12

    Because circumstances are always changing around us, the Christian life is actually a series of adjustments we make through the power of the Holy Spirit. I thought about this as I guided my fishing boat across a lake. Try as I might, I could not steer a straight course. Because of the wind and waves, I had to continually correct my steering as the boat zigzagged toward the opposite shore. We set our Christian course, but new factors always enter in. The winds of adversity and temptation may make us waver and we must keep correcting our steering. Paul's walk with Christ brought him through a variety of trials, yet his steadfastness kept him pressing toward the goal. As we travel on life's pathway, let's keep making the adjustments to stay on course. —DCE

FEBRUARY 10

[Abraham] was looking forward to the city with foundations, whose architect and builder is God. —Hebrews 11:10

When Bill Bright, founder of Campus Crusade for Christ, contracted pulmonary fibrosis, he used his time of quiet reflection during his illness to write a book called *The Journey Home*. Regarding his impending death, Bright wrote, "Knowing that heaven is our real home makes it easier to pass through the tough times here on earth. The perils of a journey on earth will be nothing compared to the glories of heaven."

Abraham illustrates this same otherworldly orientation: Although he lived in tents in the land promised to him and his family, "he was looking forward to the city with foundations, whose architect and builder is God" (Hebrews 11:9-10). A traveling foreigner, he sought—by faith—an eternal city constructed by God. Whether death is near or far away, let's exhibit a faith that focuses on our eternal home. —DF

NOVEMBER 21

He himself is our peace, who has made the two groups one and has destroyed the barrier, the dividing wall of hostility. —Ephesians 2:14

The Roman emperor Hadrian is remembered for building an eighty-mile-long wall to keep people out. In contrast, Jesus Christ is remembered for tearing down a spiritual wall to let people in.

When the early church experienced tension between Jewish and non-Jewish believers, Paul told them they stood equally in the family of God. "[Jesus] is our peace, who has made the two groups one and has destroyed . . . the dividing wall of hostility. . . . For through Him we both have access to the Father by one Spirit" (Ephesians 2:14–18). One of the most beautiful aspects of the Christian faith is the unity among those who follow Jesus. Through His death on the cross, Christ removed the barriers and has drawn us together in true friendship and love. —DCM

FEBRUARY 11

The message they heard was of no value to them, because they did not share the faith of those who obeyed. —Hebrews 4:2

A 1960s song called "Desert Pete" tells of a thirsty cowboy who finds a hand pump. It had jar of water next to it, with a note. The note warned travelers to use the jar water to prime the pump—not to drink. Obedience led to abundant cool water.

Think of Israel's journey through the wilderness. When their thirst became overwhelming (Exodus 17:1–7), God told Moses to strike a rock with his staff. Moses obeyed and water gushed from the stone. Sadly, Israel would not consistently follow Moses' example of faith. Ultimately "the message they heard was of no value to them, because they did not share the faith of those who obeyed" (Hebrews 4:2).

Sometimes life can seem like an arid desert. But God can quench our spiritual thirst in unlikely circumstances if we obey His Word. —DF

NOVEMBER 20

But when he saw the wind, he was afraid and, beginning to sink, cried out, "Lord, save me!"
—Matthew 14:30

Looking up is what kept Peter from nearly drowning when he stepped into the sea. But when he moved his eyes from the Lord to himself and the angry waves around him, he began to sink (Matthew 4:29–30). We can be just like him! Instead of resting on the Word of God and its promises, we start viewing the boisterous billows of life, the treacherous winds of adversity, and our own inadequacy to cope with our problems. The result? We panic. As soon as we look at anything else but the Lord and His Word, and try to go by our feelings, we are bound to sink beneath the waves of circumstances. The essential thing is to keep looking up—to keep our eyes on Jesus.

Don't endanger your spiritual equilibrium. Keep looking up! —HGB

FEBRUARY 12

[The LORD] refreshes my soul. —Psalm 23:3

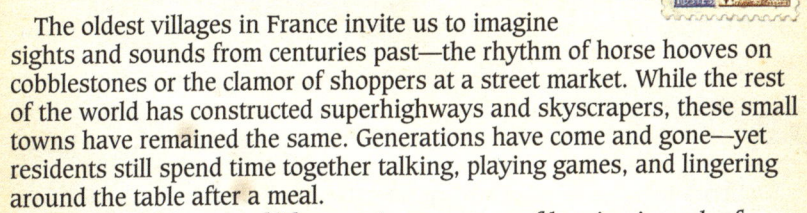

The oldest villages in France invite us to imagine sights and sounds from centuries past—the rhythm of horse hooves on cobblestones or the clamor of shoppers at a street market. While the rest of the world has constructed superhighways and skyscrapers, these small towns have remained the same. Generations have come and gone—yet residents still spend time together talking, playing games, and lingering around the table after a meal.

Pondering this way of life can stir up a sense of longing in each of us. It seems so ideal—so capable of delivering the wholeness and rest we desire. According to David, God is the one who prepares a table for us (vv. 2, 5). He allows us to "feast on the abundance of [His] house" (Psalm 36:8). He refreshes us from the inside out, enabling us to continue on in the life He has given us. —JBS

NOVEMBER 19

Stand at the crossroads and look; ask for the ancient paths, ask where the good way is, and walk in it, and you will find rest for your souls. But you said, "We will not walk in it." —Jeremiah 6:16

Visitors in England can be confused by intersections called roundabouts. Before turning into one of these traffic circles, you have to know which lane takes you where you want to go. If you get in the wrong lane, you may end up going down the wrong road or driving in circles.

The Lord told His people Israel to consider carefully where they were going (Jeremiah 6:16). He encouraged them to follow "the good way," trusting Him as they had in the past. But they refused. Millions of people today make the same mistake. When faced with a decision of whether to live for God or themselves, they choose the wrong way. Jesus said, "I am the way and the truth and the life" (John 14:6). His way is the "good way." —DBH

FEBRUARY 13

If I go and prepare a place for you, I will come back and take you to be with me that you also may be where I am. —John 14:3

Jan and Hendrikje Kasper sailed into US waters in January 1957. Their family of twelve crowded on deck of the *Grote Beer* to catch their first glimpse of the Statue of Liberty. That initial view of Lady Liberty was exciting—and emotional. They had endured an arduous eleven-day journey from the Netherlands, but finally they had arrived at their new home.

Someday, each believer in Christ will leave this life and go to the place He has prepared for us (John 14:3). While we may experience difficulties or discomfort along the way, we look forward to the final destination. Composer Don Wyrtzen wrote a wonderful song that pictures our earthly life as a "tempestuous sea." It ends with marvelous images of being, as the title suggests, "Finally Home." What glory it will be to step on shore in our eternal home! —CHK

NOVEMBER 18

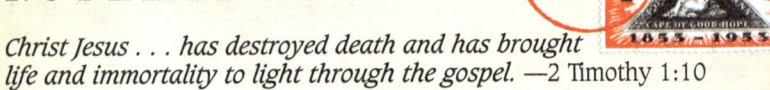

Christ Jesus . . . has destroyed death and has brought life and immortality to light through the gospel. —2 Timothy 1:10

At the southern tip of Africa, a cape jutting out into the ocean once caused sailors great anxiety. Because adverse weather so often prevailed there, the region was named the Cape of Storms. But when a Portuguese captain found a safe route through those treacherous waters, it was renamed the Cape of Good Hope.

We all face a great storm called death. But by His crucifixion and resurrection, Christ abolished eternal death for every believer and promises fellowship with Him in heaven. Although death, the "last enemy," can touch us temporarily, its brief control over our earthly body will end at the resurrection promised in 1 Corinthians 15:51–52. All who know Christ as Savior can face life's final voyage with confidence. Although the sea may be rough, the Master Helmsman has assured our safe passage. —HGB

FEBRUARY 14

The time for my departure is near. —2 Timothy 4:6

Paul's word *departure* in 2 Timothy 4:6 means "loosing" or "unmooring." It's a word he uses again when he sighs, "I am torn between the two: I desire to depart and be with Christ" (Philippians 1:23). *Departure* is a nautical term that suggests "shipping out"—weighing anchor, slipping the lines that tether us to this world and getting underway. It's a marvelous metaphor for dying. For believers in Christ, death is not an end but a beginning. It means leaving this old world behind and getting to a better place. It's a time for joy, excitement, and a hearty "Bon voyage!"

When we pass through the valley of the shadow of death, God is with us (Psalm 23:4). His hands are on the helm as He guides us to the heavenly haven He has prepared for us (John 14:1–3). —DHR

NOVEMBER 17

Cast your cares on the LORD, and he will sustain you. —Psalm 55:22

When the elevated railroad was introduced in New York City, people worried it might collapse under the weight of its passengers. But the public was assured that it "had been subjected to a most abnormal and enormous tonnage, and that consequently people of ordinary weight might deem themselves quite safe."

We can feel the same about God. The heavenly Father who promised to carry His people Israel all the way from birth to old age (Isaiah 46:3–4) promises never to leave us (Hebrews 13:5). His redemptive grace in Jesus Christ can never be overloaded, His strength never exhausted. His almighty arms can safely carry all who come to Him. In childlike faith, let's respond to the words of the psalmist and cast all our cares on the Lord (Psalm 55:22). He will never let us fall. —VG

FEBRUARY 15

They will still bear fruit in old age, they will stay fresh and green. —Psalm 92:14

If you are still young and energetic, you may not quite understand David's musings in Psalm 37:25: "I was young and now I am old." But it is an eventual reality for all of us. Because aging often brings with it pain and loss, some may vainly wish their summertime days would never end. But listen to Christian essayist and theologian F. W. Boreham: "Someday my life's little day will soften down to eventide. My sunset hours will come. . . . And then, I know there will arise, out of the dusk, a dawning fairer than any dawn that has yet broken upon me."

No matter where we are on the heavenward pilgrimage, if we are walking with Jesus we can rejoice. We know that He will abide with us till our journey on earth is over. —VG

NOVEMBER 16

This happened that we might not rely on ourselves but on God. —2 Corinthians 1:9

Yellowstone National Park fascinates me. But when I walk among the geysers, I'm aware of how close I am to danger. I am walking atop one of the largest, most active volcanoes in the world.

Job was unaware that only a hedge separated him from disaster (Job 1:9–10). When God allowed Satan to test Job, his life exploded (vv. 13–19).

Many believers live in circumstances where it seems God has removed His hedge of protection. Others live in relative calm. Like Job's friends, they assume nothing bad will happen unless they do something to deserve it. As we learn from Job, however, God sometimes allows bad things to happen to good people. Yet no disaster has the power to destroy those who trust Christ (2 Corinthians 4:8–9). Nothing can separate us from God's love. —JAL

FEBRUARY 16

Come with me by yourselves to a quiet place and get some rest. —Mark 6:31

Fifty miles west of Asheville, North Carolina, I turned off the expressway and finished my trip to the city on the scenic Blue Ridge Parkway. I drove slowly, stopping often to savor the mountain vistas and the brilliant autumn leaves. My soul was restored. I thought, "How often do I exit the fast lane of my responsibilities and concerns to focus my attention on Jesus for a time each day?"

After Jesus' disciples completed a demanding period of ministry, He said to them, "Come with me by yourselves to a quiet place and get some rest" (Mark 6:31). When their long day finally ended, Jesus sought renewal in prayer (v. 46).

Jesus is always with us whether life is hectic or calm, but there is great value in taking time each day to walk the quiet road with Him. —DCM

NOVEMBER 15

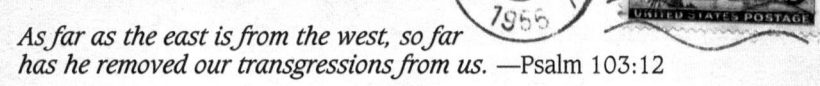

As far as the east is from the west, so far has he removed our transgressions from us. —Psalm 103:12

How far is the east from the west? A city's slogan reads: "Where the west begins, in the state where the tall corn grows." The last part of the slogan is true; the first is not. No one knows where the west begins or ends. It's all a matter of where we are. If I were in New York and wanted to travel as far west as possible, how far would I have to go? Los Angeles? The Philippines are west of there and China is further still, and so on all the way back to New York. How far west must I go to reach the east? It cannot be measured.

Rejoice! Because Jesus died on the cross and rose from the grave, God removed your sins "as far as the east is from the west" (Psalm 103:12). —MRD

FEBRUARY 17

Come to me, all you who are weary and burdened, and I will give you rest. —Matthew 11:28

After a long journey from Hong Kong, including ten hours of delays and layovers, we arrived in Chicago. We missed the last flight to Grand Rapids, so the airline arranged hotel rooms for us. We must have been a sorry sight. One hotel worker looked at us and simply said, "Distressed travelers." It felt appropriate after two hard days of travel.

That's a good metaphor for life. We are pilgrims in this world, traveling to a heavenly home beyond description. Along the way, cares and burdens rob us of our hope and joy. We become distressed travelers. The Lord offers, "Come to me, all you are weary and burdened, and I will give you rest" (Matthew 11:28).

Distressed in your journey? Lean on Him! His love and care are there to restore your heart. —BC

NOVEMBER 14

To me, to live is Christ and to die is gain. . . .
I am torn between the two: I desire to depart and
be with Christ. —Philippians 1:21-23

As Christians, we are pulled in two directions. We want to go to heaven, but this life also holds great appeal. We don't need to feel guilty for having a strong desire to enjoy life. Marriage, a family, a fulfilling job—all have a legitimate appeal. But if the delights of our earthly home are so attractive that we lose sight of God's purpose for putting us here, something's wrong.

The apostle Paul had mixed feelings too. The looming possibility of his death created a conflict. He longed to be with Christ, for that would be "better by far" (Philippians 1:23). He also wanted to live; his fellow believers needed him (v. 24). Paul was pulled in two directions, and in both cases it was for the highest reason. What about us? —DD

FEBRUARY 18

I am the LORD, who heals you.
—Exodus 15:26

    After the Israelites miraculously crossed the Red Sea, they were led into the desert. God wanted to show them that life is a combination of bitter and sweet, triumph and defeat. When the Israelites arrived at Marah, they complained because the water was bitter (Exodus 15:23). After Moses interceded (v. 25), God reminded them to keep His commandments (v. 26). Then He brought them to the refreshment of Elim (v. 27). God was involved in their daily affairs. He wanted them to know that He not only could part the sea, but He would also supply water for His people.

    Are you in the wilderness of disappointment and bitterness right now? Trust God. He will lead you out of the desert and into a place of spiritual abundance, healing, and refreshment. —MW

NOVEMBER 13

I am already being poured out like a drink offering, and the time for my departure is near. —2 Timothy 4:6

    During his final days on earth, the apostle Paul longed for his heavenly home. Although he was facing death, thoughts of heaven and the warm welcome he would receive from the Lord kept him hopeful (2 Timothy 4:8). This reminds me of an old man and his grandson who were sitting on a dock late one afternoon. The two chatted about everything, it seemed. Finally the boy asked, "Grandpa, does anybody ever see God?" "Son," said the old man as he looked across the lake, "it's getting so now I hardly see anything else."

    Aging should be like that. Praying should come more easily. Communion with the Father in heaven should be as natural as breathing. Thoughts of seeing Jesus and going home should increasingly occupy our minds. That's how we'll know we're ready to go home. —HR

FEBRUARY 19

A Samaritan, as he traveled, came where the man was; and when he saw him, he took pity on him.
—Luke 10:33

A Samaritan made his way to Jericho and encountered a wounded Jew lying beside the road. Others had hurried by, too busy to stop. But the Samaritan, hated by the Jews, "took pity." He "bandaged his wounds, . . . and took care of him" (Luke 10:33–34).

God's will sometimes comes to us in the form of interruptions. Just when we think our duties are done for the day and we've settled in for a quiet evening, someone calls or texts, asking for our time. Maybe we should not see these intrusions as interruptions. We can see them as opportunities God is sending us to serve others—to listen, to show love, to help them on their journey with God. "Who is my neighbor?" I ask. Jesus answers, "The person in need I'm sending your way." —DHR

NOVEMBER 12

First go and be reconciled to [your brother or sister]; then come and offer your gift. —Matthew 5:24

How far would you travel to put things right with a brother who hadn't spoken to you in 10 years? Alvin Straight decided it was time to end the silence and break down the wall of anger he and his brother had built between them. Unable to drive a car and despising bus travel, this 73-year-old man drove 300 miles . . . on a lawn mower!

Jesus said, "If you are offering your gift at the altar and there remember that your brother or sister has something against you, leave your gift there in front of the altar. First go and be reconciled to them; then come and offer your gift" (Matthew 5:23–24). Is there someone with whom you need to make things right? Why not go to that person and do it today? —DCM

FEBRUARY 20

*Zaccheaus, come down immediately.
I must stay at your house today.* —Luke 19:5

Every time my family arrived at the door of my grandparents' West Virginia farmhouse, Grandma Lester greeted us with, "Come on in and sit a spell." It was her way of telling us to make ourselves comfortable, stay a while, and share in some "catching up" conversation.

In our busy world, it's tough to find time to ask someone to "Sit a spell." But look at what Jesus did when He wanted to get into the life of a tax collector. He went to Zacchaeus's house. To share His heart properly with Zacchaeus, Jesus knew He would have to spend quality time talking to Him. His words, "I must stay at your house" indicate that this was no quick stopover.

If we are going to get into someone's life to make a difference—as Jesus did for Zacchaeus—we need to ask others to "Come sit a spell." —DB

NOVEMBER 11

My days are swifter than a weaver's shuttle, and they come to an end without hope. —Job 7:6

On a cloudless summer day, a man lying on his back in a quiet park may feel as though all time and movement have stopped under the hot rays of the sun. Yet our Milky Way galaxy is hurtling through space at 1.3 million miles per hour! And just as we are hurtling through the heavens at unimaginable speeds, we are also moving from here to eternity. Our days and opportunities to live for the Lord pass so rapidly that we cannot afford to waste any of them.

The psalmist prayed, "Teach us to number our days, that we may gain a heart of wisdom" (Psalm 90:12). May that be our prayer today. Lord, help us to live without desperation or futility as we quickly travel from our home here on earth to our heavenly home above. —MD

FEBRUARY 21

He guided them to their desired haven. —Psalm 107:30

Psalm 107 tells of those who "went out on the sea in ships" (v. 23). Along their journey at sea, they see God as the One behind the tempestuous storm and the One who calms it. In the world of sailing vessels there were two great fears. One fear was of a terrible gale, and the other was of having no wind at all.

Sometimes life demands that we weather a storm. At other times it puts us to the test of tedium. We may feel stuck. But whether we find ourselves in a crisis of circumstance or in a place where the spiritual wind has been taken out of our sails, we need to trust God for guidance. The Lord, who is sovereign, will eventually guide us to our desired haven (v. 30). —DF

NOVEMBER 10

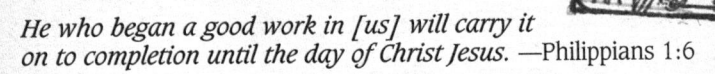

*He who began a good work in [us] will carry it
on to completion until the day of Christ Jesus.* —Philippians 1:6

One day Billy and Ruth Graham were driving through a long stretch of road construction. When they finally reached the end, a sign caught Ruth's attention: "End of construction. Thanks for your patience." She commented that those words would be a fitting inscription on her gravestone someday.

When we accept Jesus Christ as Savior and Lord, we begin the lifelong process of spiritual growth. We're "under construction." The Holy Spirit works in us to remove our selfishness (Philippians 2:4), to renew our thinking (Romans 12:2), and to develop Christlike qualities in us (Colossians 3:5–14). Paul assures us that "He who began a good work in [us] will carry it on to completion until the day of Christ Jesus" (Philippians 1:6). "We shall be like him" (1 John 3:2), perfectly conformed to our Savior's likeness. —VG

FEBRUARY 22

I strike a blow to my body and make it a slave. —1 Corinthians 9:27

A man was traveling on an unpaved road when melting snow made it nearly impossible to drive. He saw a sign that said, "Take care which rut you choose. You will be in it for the next 25 miles." That's a wise warning! Which ruts of routine are we establishing?

A habit is a pattern of behavior we follow consistently. We need to decide prayerfully what habits we will practice. Will our habits be ruts of routine—or "grooves of grace"? Paul referred to his life's journey as a race. He said the only way to stay the course was to "discipline [his] body and bring it into subjection" (1 Corinthians 9:27 NKJV).

Good health habits are important, but spiritual disciplines—habits of prayer, Bible reading, and kindness—are far more important. Spiritual discipline transforms our ruts into grooves of grace. —VG

NOVEMBER 9

May I never boast except in the cross of our Lord Jesus Christ. —Galatians 6:14

Travelers who drive through Groom, Texas, are surprised by the sight of a giant cross. That symbol of the Christian faith was erected in the hope that anyone who sees it might turn to Jesus. We're grateful when a nonbeliever's attention is drawn to Jesus Christ and the cross, for who can predict what even a split-second reaction may mean? Suddenly a sinful person may begin to wonder why Jesus died on the cross, and this may prompt her to seek answers.

What about us? As we hurry along life's often-dreary landscape, are we grateful for reminders of our Father's love? Through the cross, Jesus has reconciled us to God and given us His peace (Ephesians 2:14–16). Take some time today to reflect on the meaning of the cross, and let it flood your heart with praise. —VG

FEBRUARY 23

These commandments that I give you today are to be on your hearts. —Deuteronomy 6:6

When I was in high school, a driving instructor gave me these wise words: "When you look in the rearview mirror, you think you know what's on your left, but your vision is limited. Always check your blind spot!" This has kept me out of many potential accidents.

Moses had wise instruction for the people of Israel: Make the study of God's commandments an integral part of life. Moses said, "Impress them on your children. Talk about them when you sit at home and when you walk along the road" (Deuteronomy 6:7). God's words were to permeate every aspect of their lives. Just as checking our blind spot should be automatic while we drive, so applying God's Word should be our natural response as we encounter life's hazards. —DF

NOVEMBER 8

The heavens are the work of your hands.
—Psalm 102:25

In 1977, the United States launched a rocket into space. On board was a small craft called Voyager I, a probe jettisoned into space to explore the planets. Decades later, that tiny vehicle was still going—traveling at a speed of over 38,000 miles per hour, nearly 9 billion miles from the sun. That's mind-boggling!

But it's nothing when compared with what God has done. We have barely begun to explore the vastness of God's creation. Yet every small step by humankind should put us in absolute awe of God's power and creativity. Think of this: While we have left the realm of one star with a spaceship, the Creator of the stars "calls forth each of them by name" (Isaiah 40:26). Exploring the universe is amazing. But exploring the God who made it all: That's beyond amazing! —DB

FEBRUARY 24

I will never leave you nor forsake you. —Joshua 1:5

My friend Ralph had the thrilling experience of going on a short cruise on the aircraft carrier USS *John F. Kennedy*. He was told that whenever the planes are taking off or landing the captain watches from the bridge. Each time a pilot takes off or lands on the deck, he knows that his captain is on duty.

When it was time for Joshua to take over as leader of Israel, he needed reassurance that God would be with him as He had been with Moses. God promised him, "As I was with Moses, so I will be with you" (Joshua 1:5). Joshua could lead Israel with confidence that God was always watching over him.

Whatever spiritual battle we may face, we know God is with us. He guides, protects, and leads us. He's always on the bridge! —DCE

NOVEMBER 7

If you possess these qualities in increasing measure, they will keep you from being ineffective and unproductive in your knowledge of our Lord Jesus Christ. —2 Peter 1:8

On a recent trip, my wife sat near a mother with a young boy on his first flight. Throughout the flight, the boy remained glued to the window, absorbed in the wonder of all he was seeing.

For "experienced travelers" in the Christian life, there can be great danger in losing the wonder of God and of the Scriptures that once thrilled us. Peter urged the early followers of Christ to continue growing in godly character (2 Peter 1:5–7). He said, "If you possess these qualities in increasing measure, they will keep you from being ineffective and unproductive in your knowledge of our Lord Jesus Christ" (v. 8). Without them, we forget the marvel of being cleansed from our sins (v. 9). May God grant us grace to keep growing in the wonder of knowing Him. —DCM

FEBRUARY 25

Make level paths for your feet, so that the lame may not be disabled, but rather healed.
—Hebrews 12:13

In a way, all Christians are road builders—paving the way of faith for the next generation. The faithfulness of our lives may determine how difficult their journey will be. Will they have to repair the damage we have done to the road? Will they be able to build new roads for others to find the way to God? To be good road builders, we must heed biblical advice. The author of Hebrews instructed us to live in peace and be holy (12:14), to make sure no one misses the grace of God, and not to permit bitterness to grow and cause trouble (v. 15).

Let's remember those who will follow us by practicing our faith in a way that makes it easy for others to come to Jesus. What kind of road builder are you? —JAL

NOVEMBER 6

The LORD was with him; he showed him kindness and granted him favor. —Genesis 39:21

Joseph landed in prison for a crime he didn't commit (Genesis 39). Abandoned and forgotten by anyone who might help, he was stranded. Still, "the LORD was with him; . . . showed him kindness and granted him favor" (v. 21). Eventually, the prison warden promoted Joseph to oversee fellow inmates, and whatever Joseph did, God "gave him success" (v. 23). But despite God's presence and blessing, Joseph remained incarcerated for years.

You may be stranded in a hospital room, a jail cell, a country far from home, or your own inner prison. No matter where you are, or how long you've been there, God's mercy and kindness can reach you. Because He is God Almighty (Exodus 6:3) and present everywhere (Jeremiah 23:23–24), He can protect and provide for you when it seems no one else can help. —JBS

FEBRUARY 26

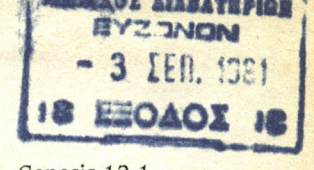

Go from your country, your people and your father's household to the land I will show you. —Genesis 12:1

Our lives are subject to detours and corrections that we never expected or imagined. Abraham and Sarah would agree. They were planning for retirement when life "happened" to them. God adjusted their agenda. He told Abraham, "Go from your country, your people and your father's household to the land I will show you" (Genesis 12:1). So this old couple packed up the tent and headed out to only God knew where. God gave Abraham and Sarah marching orders without a map. They needed only enough faith to begin the journey, and they headed out to unknown territories and unimagined adventures.

Make your plans. But write them on paper and keep an eraser handy. God and life have a way of leading you on a journey that you might not have anticipated in your wildest dreams. —HR

NOVEMBER 5

Become blameless and pure, "children of God without fault in a warped and crooked generation." Then you will shine among them like stars in the sky as you hold firmly to the word of life. —Philippians 2:15–16

Prior to the American Civil War (1861–1865), many fugitive slaves found freedom by following the Underground Railroad. They traveled at night, keeping on track by following the light of the "Drinking Gourd," a code name for the collection of stars known as the Big Dipper. The "drinking gourd" served as a point of light directing the slaves to freedom. The apostle Paul says that believers are to shine "like stars in the sky" to show the way to those seeking God's truth, redemption, and spiritual liberation (Philippians 2:15). We live in a dark world that desperately needs to see the light of Jesus Christ. Our calling is to shine forth God's truth so that others can be directed to Jesus, the One who is the way, the truth, and the life (John 14:6). —DF

FEBRUARY 27

For here we do not have an enduring city, but we are looking for the city that is to come. —Hebrews 13:14

In wintertime, a condition known as a "whiteout" sometimes occurs along the Lake Michigan shoreline. The air becomes so filled with powdery snow that you can't see more than a few feet ahead. If you're driving, you feel totally helpless. I recall heading back toward Grand Rapids on a cold, snowy day. It was after dark, and the situation continually grew worse. Suddenly, we were enveloped by a brief whiteout. It was frightening! After a slow, tedious journey, we finally pulled into our driveway. I think every member of the family said, "I'm sure glad to get home!"

I wonder if we'll have a similar feeling when we enter heaven. The dangerous "whiteouts" of our earthly journey—temptations, stresses, and failures—will be over. Best of all, we'll be safe with our Savior. We'll be so glad to get home! —DCE

NOVEMBER 4

But he knows the way that I take; when he has tested me, I will come forth as gold. —Job 23:10

Many years ago I visited a remote mission in the hills. My means of transportation for the last three miles was an old skinny mule. As the missionary helped me into the saddle, he said, "Don't use the reins, and don't try to guide the mule. He knows this road much better than you do." It was pitch dark and so I trusted that the mule knew the way. The next day the missionary took me back to the road we had traveled the night before. My heart skipped a beat when I saw the narrow, dangerous, rocky trail!

I learned a lesson that day. If we could see the dangers ahead we would despair, so the Lord leaves us in the dark. Let's travel on in faith, trusting the One who knows the way! —MRD

FEBRUARY 28

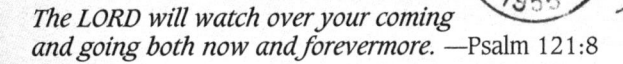

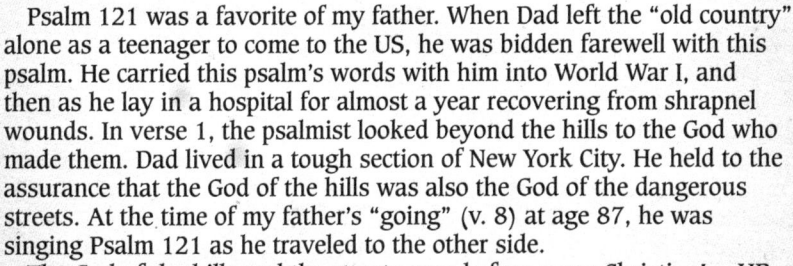

*The LORD will watch over your coming
and going both now and forevermore.* —Psalm 121:8

Psalm 121 was a favorite of my father. When Dad left the "old country" alone as a teenager to come to the US, he was bidden farewell with this psalm. He carried this psalm's words with him into World War I, and then as he lay in a hospital for almost a year recovering from shrapnel wounds. In verse 1, the psalmist looked beyond the hills to the God who made them. Dad lived in a tough section of New York City. He held to the assurance that the God of the hills was also the God of the dangerous streets. At the time of my father's "going" (v. 8) at age 87, he was singing Psalm 121 as he traveled to the other side.

The God of the hills and the streets goes before every Christian! —HR

NOVEMBER 3

Direct me in the path of your commands, for there I find delight. —Psalm 119:35

A man was looking for a new chauffeur. He gave each applicant a demanding series of road tests, one of which involved driving in a mountainous area. To impress his prospective employer, one of the drivers sped along the winding trail at high speeds, closely skirting the edge of the precipice. Another applicant, however, got the job. When asked why, the employer replied, "I wasn't interested in which one could come the closest to danger. I wanted the man who would take the 'safe path' and avoid the brink of disaster."

God also desires that we steer as far away from sin as we can. His Word tells us: "Do not set foot on the path of the wicked or walk in the way of evildoers. . . . Turn from it" (Proverbs 4:14–15). —RD

FEBRUARY 29

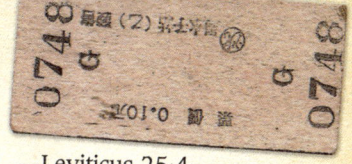

In the seventh year the land is to have a year of sabbath rest, a sabbath to the LORD. —Leviticus 25:4

The earth's solar orbit takes 365 and a quarter days. Therefore, every four years one day is added to the calendar so we don't fall behind in the cycle of things. Leap year's February 29 is that adjustment.

In ancient Israel's calendar, God set up a way to readjust things. Just as humankind was commanded to rest every seventh day (Exodus 20:8–10), so the land was to rest and restore its nutrients during the seventh year (Leviticus 25:4). With our hectic pace of life, we too need readjustment. Daily demands require reevaluation. One suggestion: Observe the sabbath principle—set aside time to rest and refocus. Jesus, for example, went "to a solitary place, where he prayed" (Mark 1:35). Is it time for readjustment? Slow down and prayerfully ask God to reset your spiritual calendar to His will. —DF

NOVEMBER 2

Here I am! I stand at the door and knock. —Revelation 3:20

Henry Wadsworth Longfellow said, "If you only knock long enough and loud enough at the gate, you are sure to wake up somebody." Ideally that *somebody* comes to the door and lets the outsider in. The act of knocking doesn't guarantee entry—entry is only possible if someone responds.

In Revelation 3:20, Jesus says to believers in Laodicea, "I stand at the door and knock." He is banging on the door of a church filled with His own followers! These believers have only a halfhearted commitment to Him (vv. 15–16). They might acknowledge Him with a friendly nod, but Jesus wants closeness, fellowship. He says, "If anyone hears my voice and opens the door, I will come in and eat with that person, and they with me" (v. 20). Is Jesus calling us into deeper fellowship with himself? We can choose to open the door to His influence every day. —JBS

MARCH 1

By faith [Abraham] made his home in the promised land like a stranger in a foreign country. —Hebrews 11:9

Now that I'm getting closer to the end of life's journey, I'm thinking more like a transient. I suppose it's natural. Abraham first described himself as "a foreigner and stranger" when he was buying a burial plot for Sarah (Genesis 23:4). Time and death make you think about such things. Most elderly believers say the same thing: The world is behind; our home is ahead.

In the new heavens and new earth, there are no valleys of weeping, for God "will wipe every tear from their eyes. There will be no more death or mourning or crying or pain, for the old order of things has passed away" (Revelation 21:4). That promise makes the present journey easier to endure. Put another way, it's the hope of going home that keeps me going. I can hardly wait to get there! —DHR

NOVEMBER 1

While they were stoning him, Stephen prayed, "Lord Jesus, receive my spirit." . . . Those who had been scattered preached the word wherever they went. —Acts 7:59; 8:4

God's children must sometimes take a seemingly unpleasant detour. All was going well in the early church when God allowed Stephen to be martyred and an outbreak of persecution to take place (Acts 7:54–8:1). I am sure many believers couldn't understand why. We know now, however, that the scattering of Christians spread the gospel.

The next time you hear of a tragedy on a mission field or in a church, just remember that this "detour" may, through the Lord's overruling providence, be used to eventually bring great blessing to others. The Savior may also permit an illness or hardship to enter your life. You may not like this turn of events, but trust Him. God may be using this detour to bring great spiritual enrichment. —HVL

MARCH 2

Who will get what you have prepared for yourself?
—Luke 12:20

We're inclined to accumulate far too many possessions on our journey through life, don't you think? We're bombarded with ads that urge us to purchase things we just can't live without. So we buy more and more and more.

The rich man in Jesus' parable (Luke 12:13–21) may have been dreaming about all the good things he could acquire because he had a great crop. He said he would build bigger barns, and he would spend his time eating, drinking, and partying. But God told him, "You fool! This very night your life will be demanded from you" (v. 20). The principle is clear: Be "rich toward God," not rich in things (v. 21). Besides, you'll have to leave it all behind when it's time to go Home. —DCE

OCTOBER 31

Follow my example, as I follow the example of Christ. —1 Corinthians 11:1

The apostle Paul assured the Corinthians that if they followed his example, it would never lead them astray. I want to be able to say the same. When a friend of mine was traveling, he stopped and asked for directions. Yet after wandering around for thirty minutes, he lost his way entirely. At a traffic signal, a car pulled up next to him. Opening the window, he asked the man for directions. He replied, "Just follow me!" In a few minutes they arrived at the desired destination.

There's a great difference between telling a person the way and showing him. You may be able to tell a man how to live the Christian life, but it is another thing to show him the way! May we be able to say with Paul, "Imitate me" (1 Corinthians 4:16). —MRD

MARCH 3

Come to me, all you who are weary and burdened, and I will give you rest. —Matthew 11:28

Salmon fascinate me. Driven by instinct, they swim against currents, up waterfalls, and around hydroelectric dams. Despite eagles, bears, and many other predators, they struggle to reach their ancestral spawning grounds to lay their eggs.

Their journey reminds me of the human journey. We too have a homing instinct. "There exists in the human mind, and indeed by natural instinct, a sense of Deity," John Calvin said. We are born and we live for the express purpose of knowing and loving God. He is the source of our life. Augustine reminds us that our hearts are restless until they come to Him.

Are you restless today, driven by discontent and a longing for that elusive "something more"? Jesus Christ is the source and satisfaction of all you seek. Come to Him. Find rest for your soul (Matthew 11:28). —DHR

OCTOBER 30

We accept human testimony, but God's testimony is greater because it is the testimony of God, which he has given about his Son. —1 John 5:9

When you stop to think about it, we all put our lives in the hands of strangers daily. Whether boarding a bus, taking a taxi, or getting on a plane, we commit ourselves to individuals who are total strangers. We also take the word of others concerning matters of health, nutrition, and finances, and act accordingly. Yet, isn't it amazing how reluctant some people are to trust the Lord and His Word? It's utterly inconsistent to place our confidence in people and then refuse to rely upon the Lord. We have good reason to believe what He says. Solomon declared, "Not one word has failed of all [his] good promises" (1 Kings 8:56).

Above everyone else, the faithful, omnipotent God of the Bible is the One you can trust! —RD

MARCH 4

Do not let sin reign in your mortal body so that you obey its evil desires. —Romans 6:12

Each journey into sin takes its toll. We sacrifice our closeness with God, forfeiting His blessing (Psalm 24:1–5), and we lose our influence on others (1 Timothy 4:12). The wild areas in us may never be fully tamed, but we can set up perimeters that keep us from wandering into them. One perimeter is to remember that we are dead to sin's power (Romans 6:1–14). We do not have to give in to it. The second perimeter is to resist temptation when it first attracts us. Don't let it gain power and overwhelm us. The third perimeter is accountability. Find a person who will commit to ask you the tough questions.

Impurity is ruinous, but if we long for holiness and ask God for help, He will give us victory. —DHR

OCTOBER 29

Do not be anxious about anything, but in every situation, by prayer and petition, with thanksgiving, present your requests to God. —Philippians 4:6

The apostle Paul gave three guidelines in Philippians 4:6 for the Christian who faces unsurmountable difficulty. First, be anxious for nothing! Worry is fruitless when we can trust in the wisdom of our heavenly Father. Second, be thankful for anything! Tight corners give us an opportunity to be grateful for all that is available through our heavenly Father's rich supply. Third, be prayerful about everything! God may allow us to get into a predicament so that we will diligently seek His face and wait upon Him.

Hard places often test us to the limit of our endurance. But when we look to the Lord, He will surely demonstrate His power and deliver us just as He did His people on the shores of the Red Sea long ago (Exodus 14:13). —PVG

MARCH 5

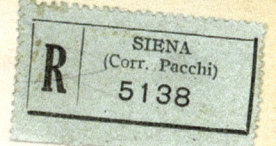

[Jesus said,] "In this world you will have trouble. But take heart! I have overcome the world." —John 16:33

There's a lake near our home that is known for good fishing. To get there, I take a mountain road I carefully mapped out. Once while driving it, I came to a section that was worse than I remembered—rocky, rutted, and steep. I stopped and checked my map. There, penciled alongside this stretch on the map, were the words: "Rough and steep. Hard going." I was on the right road.

Jesus said that our life's journey will be rough going if we choose to follow Him. "In this world you will have trouble" (John 16:33). So we shouldn't be surprised if our path becomes difficult. We can relax because Jesus said that in Him we can have peace, for He has "overcome the world" (v. 33). If you're following Christ and experiencing bumpy times, take heart—you're on the right road! —DHR

OCTOBER 28

We are confident, I say, and would prefer to be away from the body and at home with the Lord. —2 Corinthians 5:8

Walter Knight wrote of the funeral of pastor and evangelist F. B. Meyer: "London has seldom witnessed a funeral service such as was held for him. . . . The Scriptures all spoke of the Christian's hope of immortality; and Easter hymns were sung. As the organ began to play at the conclusion of the service, the vast audience rose and stood with bowed heads, waiting for the funeral march to begin. But to their surprise they heard the triumphant notes of the 'Hallelujah Chorus.' What music could have been more appropriate! A faithful soldier of the cross had been ushered into the presence of his King."

When Christian loved ones die, we can rejoice for them, though we weep for ourselves. For the child of God, death is the doorway to heaven! —RD

MARCH 6

When I am afraid, I put my trust in you. —Psalm 56:3

Few of us are free from fear. Who can testify that they always practice this verse: "In God I trust and am not afraid"? (Psalm 56:11). We do trust, yet we may be troubled by gnawing worries. Even the apostle Paul had anxieties. He confessed to the Corinthians, "I came to you in weakness with great fear and trembling" (1 Corinthians 2:3).

So don't worry that you have worries! If you are troubled by anxieties, admit it. Share them with a trusted friend. Above all, talk to the all-compassionate friend, Jesus Christ, who says, "Do not be afraid" (Luke 12:32). Ask Him for grace to overcome your fears and worries. Then "wait for the LORD; be strong and take heart" (Psalm 27:14). On your journey through life, whenever you're afraid, trust in the Lord (Psalm 56:3). —VG

OCTOBER 27

I am torn between the two: I desire to depart and be with Christ, which is better by far. —Philippians 1:23

Many people feel no need for Jesus. They live in prosperity and enjoy good health, and no adversity has forced them to reevaluate the direction they've taken. They seem oblivious to the fact that at some point their journey will bring them to the brink of eternity. What then?

Countless believers have found that when their earthly lives came to an end a glorious way was open before them. Near death, John Bunyan said, "Weep not for me, but for yourselves. I go to the Father of our Lord Jesus Christ." John Wesley said just moments before he left this earth, "The best of all, God is with us." And the apostle Paul declared, "For to me to live is Christ, and to die is gain." Receive Christ and take the road that leads to heaven. —DD

MARCH 7

Noah was a righteous man, blameless among the people of his time, and he walked faithfully with God.
—Genesis 6:9

Have you taken 10,000 steps today? It's a plan that many are using to gain better physical fitness. It's even more important to stay spiritually fit by "walking with God," which the Bible describes as an intimate, growing relationship with the Lord. "Enoch walked faithfully with God 300 years" (Genesis 5:22). "Noah was a righteous man, blameless among the people of his time, and he walked faithfully with God" (6:9). Both men are mentioned in Hebrews 11, where they are commended for their faith.

To walk with God, we talk with the Lord, listen to Him, and enjoy His presence. We trust His guidance when we cannot see what lies ahead.

There's no better time than now to begin walking with God, because each day every step counts. —DCM

OCTOBER 26

But grow in the grace and knowledge of our Lord and Savior Jesus Christ. To him be glory both now and forever! Amen. —2 Peter 3:18

A sign at the end of an airport runway reads: "Keep Moving—If you stop, you are in danger, and a danger to those flying." This reminds me of an important spiritual truth. Unless we make progress in the Christian life, we may jeopardize ourselves by slipping back into old sinful ways *and* be a source of discouragement to others. What's needed is a consistent, determined going on with the Lord, which results in growth in grace and in the knowledge of our Lord and Savior.

Like the apostle Paul, we are to "press on toward the goal" (Philippians 3:14), unwilling to settle for the status quo. Let's keep moving—for our own sake as well as the sake of others. —PVG

MARCH 8

We are hard pressed on every side, but not crushed; perplexed, but not in despair. —2 Corinthians 4:8

Explorer Samuel Hearne (1745–1792) was on an expedition in northern Canada when thieves stole most of his supplies. In his journal Hearne wrote, "The weight of our baggage being lightened, our next day's journey was more swift and pleasant."

Back in the first century, as the apostle Paul traveled from town to town proclaiming the gospel, he faced some desperate situations (2 Corinthians 4:8–10; 11:23–33). Like Hearne, he did not despair. Instead, Paul found hope by turning to the Lord.

How did you respond the last time something went wrong? Did you fall apart? If so, ask God for patience and a positive perspective to handle life's setbacks in a godly way (James 1:2–5). Ask Him for strength and wisdom. Then thank Him for working to increase your faith. —DCE

OCTOBER 25

All Scripture is God-breathed and is useful for teaching, rebuking, correcting and training in righteousness. —2 Timothy 3:16

    After a year of dodging cars at a nearby intersection, I was pleased when a traffic signal was installed. A daily ordeal became an orderly way of getting onto a busy street.

    The Scriptures too have "signals" that should control our lives. They are prohibitions against pride, envy, hatred, irreverence, and lust. When the Holy Spirit shows a red light, we should hit the brakes. And we shouldn't move into the heavy traffic of daily life until we get a green—until pride flashes to humility, envy to charity, hatred to love, irreverence to worship, and lust to purity. God's stops and starts are designed to help us. Thoughtful Christians will follow Scripture's commands as they would obey a red light at a busy intersection. —MD

MARCH 9

Direct me in the path of your commands,
for there I find delight. —Psalm 119:35

I needed to get from the upper west side of Manhattan to the lower east side—about seven miles, I figured. Taxi? Subway? Or feet? I chose to walk. Down Broadway to Central Park. Past hundreds of storefronts. Through Chinatown. Hearing the sounds. Smelling the smells. Studying the people. I felt like a part of New York City. It was well worth the time and effort.

As we travel the Christian life, we face a similar choice: Take the easy route—depending on others for instruction, shortcutting our way past a good prayer-life, or speed-reading Scripture. Or we can take the time and effort to get close to God. Why not take a long walk with God today? "Seek him with all [your] heart" (Psalm 119:2), study His Word, and obey what He says. Such a walk will be a delight! —DB

OCTOBER 24

Do nothing out of selfish ambition. . . . not looking to your own interests but each of you to the interests of the others. —Philippians 2:3–4

Most of us have observed that human selfishness often shows itself on the roadway. We're quick to blow the horn, cut off other cars, and blame other drivers. We Christians, however, should express our faith even in our driving habits. If we look out for "the interests of others" as Paul said, we will be courteous, patient, thoughtful, and law-abiding drivers.

We can't live life as if we're the only ones on the road. God's grace must be demonstrated in all our relationships. Regardless of the failures and mistakes of others, we must always look out for their needs as well as our own. Today, let's show consideration and kindness to our "fellow travelers," whether on the highway or along the road of life. —HGB

MARCH 10

Paul and his companions . . . [were] kept by the Holy Spirit from preaching the word in the province of Asia. —Acts 16:6

A young man went to seminary, determined to become a pastor. After graduation he looked unsuccessfully for a church to pastor. After two years of teaching in a Bible college, it became clear that God wanted him to be a teacher rather than a pastor.

God sometimes frustrates our own plans as we seek to determine His will. We head in one direction; He blocks our way. Finally we learn to go where He directs us. Paul experienced this during his second missionary journey. After being "kept by the Holy Spirit from preaching the word in . . . Asia" (Acts 16:6), Paul learned that God wanted him to preach in Macedonia (vv. 9–10).

Is God frustrating your plans? He may be trying to lead you. Be sensitive to His guidance. —DCE

OCTOBER 23

Your word is a lamp for my feet, a light on my path. —Psalm 119:105

    If you've ever carried a lantern on a dark road, you know you can't see more than one step ahead. But as you take that step, the lamp moves forward and another step becomes plain. It's amazing that you can reach your destination in safety without once walking in darkness. You have light the entire way, though it's only enough for one step at a time.

    What a beautiful illustration of how God guides His children through life. We don't have to see beyond what God shows us today. He leads us, and we are assured of reaching our destination. When we simply follow His leading, we have enough light for each step of the way. Isn't it wonderful to be directed by Him? —RD

MARCH 11

Wait for the LORD; be strong and take heart and wait for the LORD.
—Psalm 27:14

    Do we ever see Jesus in a hurry? This man had just three years from His first miracle at a wedding to His ascension to heaven to set in motion a revolution. Yet we never see Him running to His next healing or rushing along the streets of Capernaum. He never tells the disciples to row the boat faster.

    Jesus took His time. When He got word that His friend Lazarus was sick, "he stayed where he was two more days" (John 11:6). He paused on His way to Jairus's house to speak with the woman who touched His garment (Mark 5:21–42). There seemed to be no urgency. What can we learn from Jesus? Slow down. "Be still, and know that I am God" (Psalm 46:10) and "Wait for the LORD" (Psalm 27:14). —DB

OCTOBER 22

Do not set foot on the path of the wicked or walk in the way of evildoers. Avoid it, do not travel on it; turn from it and go on your way. —Proverbs 4:14–15

Several artists were asked to illustrate the concept of temptation. Some pictured humanity's struggle against the alluring desires of the flesh, but the prize-winning canvas was quite different. It portrayed a pastoral scene in which a man walked a country lane among inviting shade trees and lovely wild flowers. In the distance the way divided into two roads. The artist was indicating that sin's allurements are subtle at first—just an innocent fork in the road! The path that veers to the wrong seems just as inviting as the one that keeps to the right.

We must beware of taking that first easy step when we face temptation. The seemingly harmless "fork in the road" may lead down to "the path of the wicked." —HGB

MARCH 12

You give them drink from your river of delights. For with you is the fountain of life. —Psalm 36:8–9

Seeking respite from London's urban frenzy, crowds gravitate to Surrey's Loseley Park. Yet even in the gardens, the din of life can obscure nature's subtle music. People who press past distraction hear a quiet sound—a fountain, spilling water into a pool reflecting spring's soft shades.

There's something about water! Long ago, a tired rabbi rested beside a well in the midday heat and asked a woman for a drink. It was not his physical comfort he had in mind but her spiritual refreshment. "Everyone who drinks this water will be thirsty again," He told her, "but whoever drinks the water I give them will never thirst" (John 4:13–14).

Jesus, the source of living water, invites each of us to come away from the noise and listen for the calm assurance of His voice. As we turn to Him, we find perpetual refreshment for our spirits. —TG

OCTOBER 21

I have fought the good fight, I have finished the race, I have kept the faith. —2 Timothy 4:7

The Christian race is not a competitive event, but an endurance run to see who finishes faithfully. It's like the experience of Bill Broadhurst, who entered a 10,000-meter race a decade after an aneurysm surgery left him partially paralyzed. Who would guess, after such a health crisis, that a man could compete in a 6.2-mile race? Sweat rolled down his face, pain pierced his ankle, but he kept going. Almost two and a half hours later, long after the other competitors, he reached the finish line.

When Jesus hung on a cross, it appeared He had lost. But three days later, the tomb was empty and death defeated. Jesus stayed true to His Father's will and finished well. We can, too. "Faithful to the finish" makes us real winners. —DD

MARCH 13

I am going there to prepare a place for you.
—John 14:2

Because my daughter is a flight attendant, I am blessed with a parent's pass for my personal use. For a small service charge, I can fly wherever the airline flies. However, I must be on "standby." I can never be certain of a seat because available space isn't guaranteed.

It's a far different situation on our journey to heaven, which begins when we trust Christ for our salvation. Because of His death and resurrection, our passage to heaven is absolutely guaranteed. Our status is not pending; there is space available! If, like Thomas in John 14:5, you sometimes wonder if and how Jesus will get you to heaven, trust in His promise, "I am going there to prepare a place for you." You can count on it! —JY

OCTOBER 20

Praise the LORD, my soul, and forget not all his benefits.
—Psalm 103:2

    Sometimes as Christians we should stop along life's road and look back. Though the way may have been winding and steep, we can see how God directed us by His faithfulness. F. E. Marsh described what Christians can see when they look back: deliverances the Lord has wrought (Deuteronomy 5:15); ways He's led (8:2); blessings He's bestowed (32:7–12); victories He's won (11:2–7); encouragement He's given (Joshua 23:14).

    Facing difficulties, we sometimes forget God's past faithfulness. We see only the detours and dangers. But look back and you'll also see the joy of victory and the presence of your traveling Companion, who has promised never to leave or forsake you. Take courage! The One who brought you this far will continue to direct you. —PVG

MARCH 14

Your hand will guide me, your right hand will hold me fast. —Psalm 139:10

One of the many exciting aspects of walking with Christ is that we don't know what's going to happen next. At times we may be uncomfortable with life's twists and turns, but God reserves the right to lead us wherever He wants.

Paul and his missionary companions were making their way through Asia Minor when God changed their plans (Acts 16:6–7). Instead of going to Bithynia, they went to Troas. That night Paul saw a vision of a man pleading, "Come over to Macedonia and help us" (v. 9). Paul's plans were changed when God revealed His.

Because He is good (25:8), we can trust God with our lives in this great adventure called the Christian life. —DCE

OCTOBER 19

The LORD makes firm the steps of the one who delights in him. —Psalm 37:23

John Wesley's carriage was stuck in the mud. Scheduled to preach in the next town, he was upset by the delay. But as helpers tried to free the carriage, another Christian came by. Wesley recognized the man was troubled. A crop failure had left him destitute, and he needed twenty shillings to pay his family's rent. "I believe we can supply that," Wesley said. "The Lord evidently wanted me to meet you." "Now I see why our carriage got stuck," Wesley exclaimed to his companions. "Our steps were halted so we might help that needy family."

Sometimes we have delays or travel paths we hadn't planned. Perhaps the Lord has a job for us to do. These stops are never accidental! —HGB

MARCH 15

These stones are to be a memorial to the people of Israel forever. —Joshua 4:7

I can look back at the inside cover of my "growing up" Bible—a tattered old KJV—and see two poignant scribblings from my youth. One reads, "This Book will keep you from sin, or sin will keep you from this Book." The other says, "God's will is also my will. Whatever He says to do, that's what I'll do." They are like the Israelites' stones of remembrance placed by the Jordan River. Those rocks were to remind their children of the providence of God as He guided the Hebrew people into the land of promise. Like those stones, the statements I penned in my Bible long ago keep calling me back to important truths.

Thank God today for the great truths of the Bible that keep calling you closer to Him. Consider them your stones of remembrance. —DB

OCTOBER 18

Direct my footsteps according to your word; let no sin rule over me. —Psalm 119:133

When my wife and I prepare for a trip, one of the first things we do is grab the road atlas. We study it intensely to learn the best routes, determine the number of miles we'll have to travel, pick out interesting places to visit, decide how far we can get in a day, and estimate expenses. On the journey, the atlas is our constant companion, and we consult it many times a day.

For the Christian journey, the Bible is an atlas—but also much more. It's described as a lamp (Psalm 119:105), water (Ephesians 5:26), a sword (Ephesians 6:17), food (Hebrews 5:12), milk (1 Peter 2:2), and a mirror (James 1:23). We can't do without it. —DCE

MARCH 16

Blessed are those whose strength is in you,
whose hearts are set on pilgrimage. —Psalm 84:5

A book called *The Art of Pilgrimage* contains this quote: "A journey without challenge has no meaning." Is that how we view our daily lives? Or have we become so obsessed with getting beyond the struggles of everyday life that the journey is little more than a process to be endured?

Psalm 84 profiles those whose strength is in God and "whose hearts are set on pilgrimage" (v. 5). The ancient Jews experienced this as they traveled to Jerusalem to observe special feasts. The psalm paints a picture of joy in the journey, not just in reaching the destination. The Bible urges us to savor the journey that is our lives. When we find ourselves traveling a difficult road, we can resist and complain, or we can set our hearts on pilgrimage. —DCM

OCTOBER 17

But our citizenship is in heaven. And we eagerly await a Savior from there, the Lord Jesus Christ. —Philippians 3:20

    Years ago, I visited some countries behind the Iron Curtain. Visas were applied for months in advance. At the border of each country, all paperwork was examined with rigor. Scowling guards took our passports and checked them carefully. Height and weight figures were verified. Our names were checked against lists of undesirable or suspicious people. Border crossings usually took at least three hours. Finally, after the guards believed everything was in order, we were allowed to enter.

    It won't be like that when we enter heaven. Christians are privileged citizens there. When our day of arrival comes, we won't wonder about getting in. No roadblocks, no passport checks, no visa problems. We'll be welcomed because our citizenship is already there. —DCE

MARCH 17

Jonah ran away from the LORD and headed for Tarshish. —Jonah 1:3

An elderly follower of Christ told me about her personal journey with the Lord. At one time, after a couple of terms of missionary work, she lost her enthusiasm. But God did not let her just sail away from Him. As He did with Jonah, the Lord caught her attention and drew her back to himself. She returned to serving Him willingly and joyfully.

Any person who serves the Lord can face the temptation to "walk out" on God. We can let our hearts grow cold, and we can silence our ears to the Holy Spirit's voice. Right now the Lord may be calling you back to himself. If so, fall on your knees and cry out to God. Let Him know that you've torn up your ticket to Tarshish and that you're returning to Him.
—DCE

OCTOBER 16

I have fought the good fight, I have finished the race, I have kept the faith. —2 Timothy 4:7

At one time, Mickey Thompson was one of auto racing's most recognized names. His team built the fastest cars on the track, but though they often took the lead, they never won. Why? Every car broke down during the race. Thompson made fast cars, but he couldn't build them to last. They were not good finishers.

As we run the race of life, we need to end well. The apostle Paul did. At the close of his life, he could say with confidence, "I have kept the faith" (2 Timothy 4:7). What about you? Has anything stalled you in your Christian growth? Confess your sins, make the necessary repairs, and get back into the race. If you don't give up, Jesus will help you finish well. —DCE

MARCH 18

As God has said: "I will live with them and walk among them, and I will be their God, and they will be my people." —2 Corinthians 6:16

One summer day my daughter and I were enjoying the slides and tube runs at a waterpark. While waiting in line for one of the rides, I realized that I didn't really know where the line was heading. It didn't make any difference. It was a dad-and-daughter day and we were having a good time. It wasn't important where we were going; it was being together that mattered.

That caused me to ponder my attitude toward what we often call "walking with the Lord." Are we so worried about where we're headed in life that we fail to enjoy being with Him? Isn't our life of faith more a matter of companionship than getting somewhere? We may not know where life's road will take us, but we can enjoy the journey if we are walking with our Lord. —DCM

OCTOBER 15

Do not be amazed at this, for a time is coming when all who are in their graves will hear his voice and come out—those who have done what is good will rise to live, and those who have done what is evil will rise to be condemned. —John 5:28–29

I once saw a graveyard with a striking feature. On an adjoining gravel road was a sign saying, Dead End. What a graphic reminder of how some view life! To them, death ends all. Yet if that's true, Jesus was either ignorant or deceitful. He said "all who are in their graves will hear his voice and come out." Then He made an important distinction: Some will come forth to the resurrection of life and some to the resurrection of condemnation. Those who accept Jesus' forgiveness in this life will enter heaven; those who don't will be separated from Christ.

Is death a dead end? No. Jesus lived and died to provide eternal life for all who trust Him as Savior. Does that include you? —DD

MARCH 19

I have sought your face with all my heart. —Psalm 119:58

The two most important transactions in my life happened twelve years apart. The first was when trusted Jesus as my Savior. The second was when I stood with my best friend before a church congregation and married her. Imagine how odd if after we said our wedding vows Sue and I had said, "Okay, that's it. We made the decision. We don't need to nurture our relationship." Think about that other transaction—the one you also made if you are a Christian. After you trusted Christ, wouldn't it be a shame if you did nothing else for the relationship?

Salvation is the first step in a journey of a lifetime. We must talk with Him, grow in our knowledge of Him, and increase in our love for Him. How's your relationship with the Lord today? —DB

OCTOBER 14

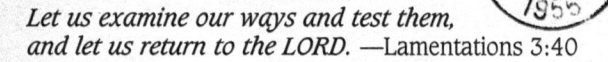

*Let us examine our ways and test them,
and let us return to the LORD.* —Lamentations 3:40

On a drive in the mountains outside Denver, I turned onto a road that went down, I thought, toward the city. But before long it changed direction, started to climb, and led away from town. I shifted into reverse, turned around, and went back to where I'd made the wrong turn.

As followers of Christ, we sometimes do or say things that take us off the path of faithful obedience to Jesus. It may be an angry argument or a deliberate choice to disobey. Then we're off-track, frustrated, and drifting farther away from Him. Before we can progress spiritually, we must confess our sin.

Is unconfessed sin keeping you from moving forward? If so, back up to go ahead. —DCE

MARCH 20

In all your ways submit to him, and he will make your paths straight. —Proverbs 3:6

My college basketball coach Don Callan was on a mission trip in Nepal. While a colleague did some work in Kathmandu, Don flew to Pokhara, praying for God's guidance. Don had been given the name of a guide in Pokhara, but no one knew Don would be visiting there. When he arrived, he walked into the lobby of a hotel. A group of men was standing at the desk, so Don ventured over and said, "I'm looking for Jeevan." What a surprise when one of the men said, "I'm Jeevan." Obviously, God had directed Don's path.

We do not always see God's guidance so clearly, but God does direct our lives. He led Isaac to Rebekah (Genesis 24), and He leads us as well. As we walk by faith on our earthly journey, we can trust God. He is our true guide. —DB

OCTOBER 13

If you declare with your mouth, "Jesus is Lord," and believe in your heart that God raised him from the dead, you will be saved. —Romans 10:9

Under the headline "Car Lover Buried in Corvette," a newspaper story began, "If there is a highway to heaven, George Swanson may get to the Pearly Gates in style. He was buried in his white Corvette."

There is a highway to heaven, but you can't travel it in a car. You get on this highway by placing trust in Jesus Christ. He died for sin, broke the power of death by His resurrection, lives in heaven as our Advocate . . . and puts all who trust Him as Savior and Lord on the highway to heaven. The highway to heaven starts on this side of death, and the entrance is easy to find: "Everyone who calls on the name of the Lord will be saved" (Romans 10:13). —HVL

MARCH 21

I will dwell in the house of the LORD forever. —Psalm 23:6

Sometimes our journey as followers of Christ is like a difficult drive through a snowy winter's night as we battle the elements with every fiber of our being to get home. In life, we struggle through long periods of hard work and difficulty. We think about home—about those wonderful passages of the Bible that describe the new heaven and the new earth. It heartens us to think of finally entering the safety of the Lord's presence.

In C. S. Lewis' wonderful story The Chronicles of Narnia, he describes the unicorn's first glimpse of heaven. He exclaims, "I have come home at last! This is my real country! I belong here. This is the land I've been looking for all my life." In a small way, that expresses how we will feel when we reach our forever home. —DCE

OCTOBER 12

Small is the gate and narrow the road that leads to life, and only a few find it. —Matthew 7:14

    Roads are everywhere. Crisscrossing the landscape, taking us wherever we want to go. And there's another thoroughfare taking us to never-before traveled areas—the "information superhighway," our avenue to discovery and knowledge. Asphalt and concrete roads lead us to physical destinations. Computer highways take us to places of the mind. All those roads. All those decisions. All those possibilities.

    Yet no road or computer network can compare with the only true superhighway—the narrow way Jesus described in Matthew 7. It's the path we take when we put our faith in Him. It is the road to heaven. Are you on that highway? We have so many paths to take in life, but God's way is the only one that leads to eternal life. —DB

MARCH 22

Let us run with perseverance the race marked out for us, fixing our eyes on Jesus. —Hebrews 12:1–2

    The trip from Magadan, Siberia, to Grand Rapids, Michigan, seemed to take forever. In actuality it took thirty hours, four stops, three different airplanes, and one border entry. What helped me endure this tiring journey was focusing on the end of the trip—my arrival home.

    The journey to spiritual maturity is also a long one. The road ahead seems endless at times as we run the race. When the way is difficult and dangerous, we tire. It seems as if there is no rest for our weary souls. That's why we must be like Abraham, who focused on the promised destination (Hebrews 11:8–10). When we remember where we are going and that Christ awaits us, we can endure anything along the way. —DCE

OCTOBER 11

*All Scripture is . . . useful for teaching,
rebuking, correcting and training in righteousness.*
—2 Timothy 3:16

I was driving near Orlando, searching for the town of Zellwood. I'd carefully located it on the map, but discovered I was on an unfamiliar road. A glance at the compass attached to my windshield, however, assured me I was headed in the right direction.

The Bible is our map. Paul assured Timothy that Scripture lays out the route of sound doctrine and righteousness (2 Timothy 3:16). But where is the compass in this passage? The compass is the Holy Spirit's work in Paul's life (vv. 10, 14). Because Timothy carefully followed Paul's Spirit-led example, he didn't lose his way. If we follow that example, neither will we. —DD

MARCH 23

The LORD is good to all; he has compassion on all he has made. —Psalm 145:9

For those who are near the end of life, are lonely or depressed, or whose bodies are weak and disease-ravaged, it is understandable that they long for the indescribable blessings of heaven—the land of no more heartache, pain, and tears. But as Christians, we certainly must not disregard the daily mercies and the rich bounties our Father gives to us. The Bible says that God "richly provides us with everything for our enjoyment" (1 Timothy 6:17). His goodness is shown to all humankind as He "provides you with plenty of food and fills your hearts with joy" (Acts 14:17). In other words, all of us, even non-Christians, are able to enjoy much of life's goodness.

Yes, heaven awaits us, but God wants us to be glad and enjoy all His goodness as we journey homeward. —VG

OCTOBER 10

For whoever wants to save their life will lose it, but whoever loses their life for me will find it.
—Matthew 16:25

    A man habitually slept as long as he could. One day, he awoke even later than usual. Rushing through his morning routine, he raced to catch the bus, barely getting on as it pulled away. Flopping into a seat, he looked around and muttered, "Where's this bus going anyway?"
    Many people are like that. Taken up with the rush of everyday activities, they never make sure they're headed in the right direction in life. How about you? Maybe it's time to wake up and ask, "Where's my life headed?" If you're going in the wrong direction, reverse course. Confess your sin to Christ and ask forgiveness. Let Him take control (Matthew 16:24). You'll be on the road to joy and eternal life. —RD

MARCH 24

As [Isaac] looked up, he saw camels approaching. —Genesis 24:63

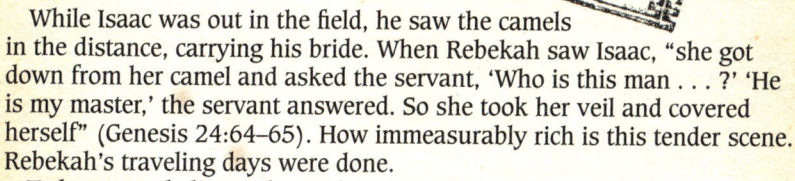

While Isaac was out in the field, he saw the camels in the distance, carrying his bride. When Rebekah saw Isaac, "she got down from her camel and asked the servant, 'Who is this man . . . ?' 'He is my master,' the servant answered. So she took her veil and covered herself" (Genesis 24:64–65). How immeasurably rich is this tender scene. Rebekah's traveling days were done.

Today we as believers have almost reached a similar point in our journey. For nearly two thousand years the Holy Spirit has been preparing the church—the Bride—and guiding her home. Soon we too will lift up our eyes, and Jesus our lover, our Savior, will break through the clouds to meet us! —MRD

OCTOBER 9

You will receive power when the Holy Spirit comes on you. —Acts 1:8

A veteran driver was explaining the axles on his truck. The front is the steering axle, while at the rear of the cab, drive axles transfer power from the engine. Our conversation reminded me of a spiritual truth. Just as steering and drive axles are essential to a tractor-trailer, so also direction and power are vital to followers of Christ. The Holy Spirit provides both. He was sent to guide us into all truth (John 16:13) and to teach us (1 Corinthians 2:10–16). We are empowered by the Spirit to witness (Acts 1:8), to pray (Romans 8:26), and to live a hope-filled life (15:13).

Next time a big semi blows by you on the highway, think of the Holy Spirit's direction and power. —DCE

MARCH 25

How beautiful are the feet of those who bring good news! —Romans 10:15

In 1983 at age sixteen, an English girl began an eleven-year trek around the world—on foot! Why did she do it? She said, "I had to discover myself." In Romans 10, Paul wrote about the feet of those who carry the gospel wherever they go (v. 15). He said that unless someone goes and tells others about Jesus, they will not hear and they will not be saved. With that in mind, we can walk with a cause—not to discover ourselves but to help others discover Christ. For this reason, God enlists our feet, even calling them beautiful!

Where will your feet be going today? How will you spread the good news about Christ? —JY

OCTOBER 8

I have calmed and quieted myself, I am like a weaned child with its mother; like a weaned child I am content. —Psalm 131:2

Life is a busy enterprise. There's always so much to do! The fast pace threatens to rob us of the quietness we need. When we're driving a car, stop signs and other signs warning us to slow down remind us we can't have our foot on the accelerator all the time. We need those reminders in all aspects of our lives.

The psalmist knew the importance of times of calm and quiet. And in the midst of His public ministry Jesus got away from the crowds and rested (Matthew 14:13). He knew it wasn't wise to accelerate through life without a break. When was the last time you said, "I have calmed and quieted myself"? (Psalm 131:2). Put up a stop sign in your busy life. Turn off the distractions that keep you from listening to God's voice. Let Him speak to you through His Word and refresh your heart and mind for His glory. —JS

MARCH 26

Those who seek the LORD lack no good thing. —Psalm 34:10

God's route to joy, happiness, and satisfaction is found in Psalm 34. In just fourteen verses, David charts a course that, when followed, leads to advantages that can be ours no matter if we are rich or poor, healthy or sick, famous or unknown. The way to happiness is marked by praising God ("I will glory in the LORD," v. 2), seeking God ("I sought the LORD, and he answered me," v. 4), fearing God ("Fear the LORD, you his holy people," v. 9), and living for God ("Turn from evil and do good; seek peace and pursue it," v. 14).

Happiness comes from going God's way. —DB

OCTOBER 7

At once they left their nets and followed him.
—Matthew 4:20

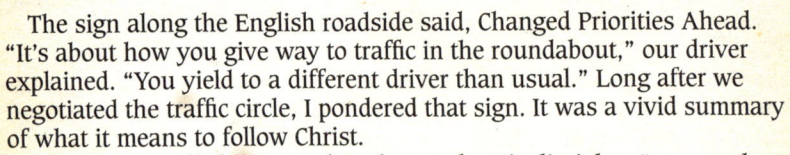

The sign along the English roadside said, Changed Priorities Ahead. "It's about how you give way to traffic in the roundabout," our driver explained. "You yield to a different driver than usual." Long after we negotiated the traffic circle, I pondered that sign. It was a vivid summary of what it means to follow Christ.

When Jesus called Peter and Andrew to be His disciples, "at once they left their nets and followed him" (Matthew 4:20). Right then, it was as if God placed a Changed Priorities Ahead sign on the road of their lives. He does the same with us. When we follow Jesus Christ, we discover that changed priorities (see Matthew 6:33, 9:9–13; Mark 9:35) are necessary to negotiate the road ahead. —DCM

MARCH 27

In Christ you have been brought to fullness. He is the head over every power and authority.
—Colossians 2:10

A poor European family that was migrating by ship to America carefully rationed some cheese and bread they brought for the journey. When a boy in the family couldn't stand another sandwich, his dad gave him their last nickel and told him to go to the ship's galley to buy an ice-cream cone. The boy returned a long time later and said, "I had three ice-cream cones and a steak dinner!" "All for a nickel?" his dad asked. "Oh, no, the food is free," the boy replied. "It comes with the ticket."

As Christians, we have been assured not only of safe passage to heaven but also of everything we need to live for Him here and now (Colossians 1:13–14; 2:6–15). Are we enjoying the abundant life he offered? Christ has all we need! —DD

OCTOBER 6

Do not worry about tomorrow,
for tomorrow will worry about itself.
—Matthew 6:34

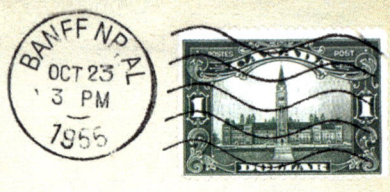

    A man was driving from the foothills of Alberta, to Banff, high in the Canadian Rockies. As the road wound westward, there always loomed a range of snow-capped peaks that seemed to block the highway. As he reached the point where it had looked as if the road would stop, he came to a sharp bend and the highway stretched on as before. Many such turns kept him progressing upward and forward until he reached the other side of the range.

    As we travel the road of life, obstacles often loom. Illness, surgery, financial reversal, or the loss of a job threatens to keep us from reaching our goals. But as we keep going by faith, God opens a new way before us. —RD

MARCH 28

*I lift up my eyes to the mountains—
where does my help come from? My help comes from the
LORD, the Maker of heaven and earth.* —Psalm 121:1–2

While visiting Colorado, I looked west to the mountains and saw a sight that filled me with wonder. Because of a layer of low, gray clouds, the foothills lay in shadows. The foothills were dark and ominous, enough to discourage any potential traveler. But beyond them, the white, snow-capped peaks of the high mountains glistened in the bright sunlight. They seemed to say, "Once you get through the shadows, you'll be all right."

How much that is like our spiritual journey! Ahead we may be able to see only the foothill shadows of hardship and trouble. The way appears difficult. Then we lift our eyes. There, gleaming afar in the sunlight, are the glorious mountain peaks of God's promises. Don't despair. Keep moving upward. Sunlit mountains lie just beyond. —DCE

OCTOBER 5

Blessed are those who fear the LORD, who find great delight in his commands. —Psalm 112:1

    I have a friend who's traveling through the fog of doubt—while he still believes God is good, much of what he's experiencing seems to contradict that. I also have an acquaintance who's reaching for God with one hand while clutching her sins in the other.

    To anyone who questions the value of walking with God, I reply: It may not be easy, but it's the only way to experience true and lasting joy. Psalm 112 declares that people who respect God and want to please Him will enjoy His favor (v. 1). That doesn't guarantee a trouble-free life, but it does assure us of peace even in tough times (vv. 6–8). We can delight in God's blessing, even when the road is hard. —JAL

MARCH 29

My help comes from the LORD, the Maker of heaven and earth. —Psalm 121:2

Psalm 121 was sung by the Hebrew pilgrims as they walked to Jerusalem to celebrate the yearly feast. The song reminded the people of the ways God took care of them. It uses four word pictures to help the pilgrims see God as the One who keeps them secure. First, He is the God of the towering hills, who gives help to His people (vv. 1–2). Second, He is the God of the night watch, who neither slumbers nor sleeps (vv. 3–4). Third, He is the God who provides friendly shade to protect from the elements that might hurt us (vv. 5–6). Fourth, He is the God of the house and of the road, who looks after us in all our comings and goings (vv. 7–8).

Keep trusting God. He keeps you in His keeping. —HR

OCTOBER 4

Trust in the LORD . . . in all your ways submit to him, and he will make your paths straight.
—Proverbs 3:5–6

   High up in a Chicago hotel, I gazed with fascination over the traffic below. One car was stalled in the midst of the traffic. From my vantage point I could see several drivers switching into the disabled car's lane, unaware of what was ahead. Thinking they were gaining time, these motorists were actually heading for greater delay.

   As we travel life's road, we do much the same thing. With our limited sight, we select the route that seems best—only to find that the temporary advance has led us into a course filled with delay and heartache. But we can look to One who is above everything and sees the whole picture. When the Lord says "stop," "change lanes," or "wait," we should gladly obey. —RD

MARCH 30

The LORD appeared to Abram and said, "To your offspring I will give this land." So he built an altar there to the LORD, who had appeared to him. —Genesis 12:7

Despite God's promises to return the people of Israel to "the land of the Canaanites" (Exodus 13:11), when they felt trapped between the Red Sea and the Egyptians, their faith failed. Turning to Moses, they said they'd rather go back to Egypt than die in the desert (Exodus 14:12). Despite their lack of faith, God saved them from the advancing army. Only then did the people fear and believe God (Exodus 14:31).

We too have promises from God. He said, "Never will I leave you" (Hebrews 13:5), yet we sometimes face our trials as if God has abandoned us. He told us, "If we ask anything according to His will, He hears us" (1 John 5:14), yet we forget to talk to Him first. During difficult times, we need to rely on God's promises. That's how faith grows strong! —DB

OCTOBER 3

It has been granted to you on behalf of Christ not only to believe in him, but also to suffer for him. —Philippians 1:29

When people tell me life is hard, I reply, "Of course it is." That answer is more satisfying than anything else I can say. The path by which God takes us often leads away from what we perceive as good. Many of us believe that if we're on the right track, God's goodness always translates into trouble-free living.

But that's far removed from the biblical perspective. God's love often leads us down roads where earthly comforts fail. Paul said, "It has been granted to you on behalf of Christ not only to believe in him, but also to suffer for him" (Philippians 1:29). When we come to the end of all our dark valleys, we'll understand that every circumstance has been allowed for our ultimate good. —DHR

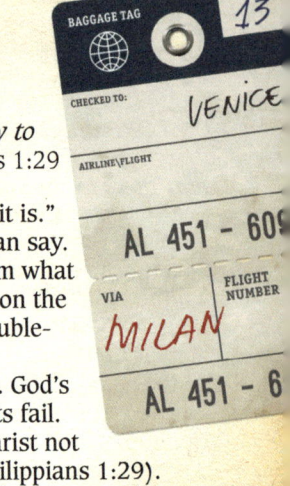

MARCH 31

Live a life worthy of the Lord and please him in every way: bearing fruit in every good work, growing in the knowledge of God. —Colossians 1:10

For nearly five years my trusty, rusty 1978 Mustang took me back and forth to work. It looked like a refugee from a junkyard, but it ran. Other drivers got to their destination with more pizzazz, but we both got there. "Just getting there" may be the only way many people can travel to work. But when it comes to how we live on the way to heaven, we all have an opportunity to travel "in style."

Paul prayed for the believers in Colosse that God would fill them "with the knowledge of his will through all the wisdom and understanding that the Spirit gives" (1:9). He wanted them to realize how spiritually rich they were in Christ (vv. 12–14). God doesn't want us just to get to heaven. He wants us to get there in style. —DB

OCTOBER 2

Prepare the way for the LORD; make straight in the desert a highway for our God. —Isaiah 40:3

As a general in World War II, Dwight D. Eisenhower had experienced the difficulty of navigating Europe's twisting roads. So, for the sake of US national security, as president he commissioned a network of roads that became the interstate highway system. Mountains were tunneled through and valleys traversed by mammoth bridges. In ancient times, conquering kings gained access to newly acquired territories through highways built for their troops. Isaiah had this in mind when he declared, "make straight in the desert a highway for our God" (Isaiah 40:3).

What would give Jesus unhindered access to your heart? Are there rough places of bitterness that need the bulldozer of forgiveness? Valleys of complaining to be filled with contentment? Let's prepare the way for the King! —JS

APRIL 1

Ship your grain across the sea; after many days you may receive a return.
—Ecclesiastes 11:1

A man dying with cancer said to me, "The life of faith is a series of adventures. I am about to experience the last and best of them as I take my journey home."

I see adventure in the opening verses of Ecclesiastes 11. The enterprising merchant engages in a venture of faith when he sends a ship out to sea loaded with merchandise. It would be away a long time, but he is willing to venture all, hoping it will return and make him a profit (v. 1).

Let's not be overly cautious because we aren't sure of the outcome. We need to invest our lives in others. We can't know if our efforts will be successful, but we'll find life adventurous. And this prepares us to face the last and best adventure of all. —HVL

OCTOBER 1

There is no other name under heaven given to mankind by which we must be saved.
—Acts 4:12

A military pilot was forced to parachute into a jungle. A local man saw what had happened and slashed through the underbrush to help. "Where's the road?" the pilot demanded. "What's the way out?" The rescuer replied, "No road! I'm the way! Follow me!" The pilot trusted the man, who led him to safety.

Some have difficulty accepting similar words of Jesus. "I am the way and the truth and the life," He said. "No one comes to the Father except through me" (John 14:6). Critics call this intolerant and divisive. But because the Son of God said it and the Word of God records it, it is true. Faith in Jesus is the only way to eternal fellowship with God. The Person is the pathway. —VG

APRIL 2

By faith Abraham, when called to go to a place he would later receive as his inheritance, obeyed. . . . For he was looking forward to the city with foundations, whose architect and builder is God. —Hebrews 11:8, 10

Abraham left his home at God's command. As he journeyed, he encountered trials. Sometimes he doubted and sometimes he failed (Genesis 15:1–6; 16:1–5). But he always returned to the path of obedience.

Life is a journey on an untraveled road. Sometimes moments of panic overwhelm us as we contemplate what lies ahead. At other times we may even turn aside because we become doubtful or we're overcome with fear. But a Christian can travel through life with calm assurance and eager anticipation. Having believed in Jesus as Savior, we have been set on a journey. If we get off course, He brings us back when we repent and confess. As we learn to trust and obey Him, we can find our way through life's detours. —HVL

SEPTEMBER 30

[God] performs wonders that cannot be fathomed, miracles that cannot be counted. —Job 5:9

Among the wonders of Jamaica is a body of water called Luminous Lagoon. If you visit there after dark, you notice that the water is filled with millions of phosphorescent organisms. Whenever there is movement, the water and the creatures in the bay glow. When fish swim past your boat, they light up like waterborne fireflies. As the boat glides through the water, the wake shines brightly.

Yet this is just a small part of the total mystery package of God's awesome handiwork as spelled out in Job 37 and 38. God's majestic creations—whether dazzling lightning or glowing fish—are mysteries to us. When we observe His creative handiwork, our only response can be that of Job: These are "things too wonderful for me" (42:3). The wonder of God's creation leaves us speechless. —DB

APRIL 3

[Jesus] said to them, "Come with me by yourselves to a quiet place and get some rest." —Mark 6:31

Some explorers in Africa hired villagers to help them on their journey through the jungle. The group set out and pushed on relentlessly for several days. Finally the guides sat down and would go no farther. When asked the reason, their leader answered, "We've been going too fast. We must pause and wait for our souls to catch up with our bodies!"

The words of Jesus to His worn-out disciples showed that He knows our human frailties. He knows that our physical and spiritual batteries need to be recharged through a time of rest and fellowship with Him. If we have no time for rest and nurturing our spiritual life, we are too busy! Sometimes God wants us to "rest a while" so our souls can "catch up" and be refreshed for the challenges that lie ahead. —HGB

SEPTEMBER 29

The Mighty One, God, the LORD, speaks and summons the earth from the rising of the sun to where it sets. —Psalm 50:1

Who has not marveled at the beauty of a sunset? We stand motionless, awestruck by the flaming sky as the sun moves over the western horizon. Seeming to hesitate a moment, the glowing orb suddenly drops out of sight, leaving the sky ablaze with brilliant shades of pink, orange, and red. Somehow the frustrations of the day are put to silence by the majestic, yet soothing voice of God as we view a glorious sunset.

To Christians, every sunset is an exclamation point given to us by God the Creator to end the day. It's as if the Lord were saying, "Set aside your worries and disappointments. Rest from your labors. I am still here, taking care of my universe. I have not changed. Look to me and be at peace." —DCE

APRIL 4

I am coming to you now, but I say these things while I am still in the world, so that they may have the full measure of my joy within them. —John 17:13

When I first went sailing with my friend Ken, I saw the sailboat as a means of transportation—like driving to work. I thought our purpose was to get to the next destination as fast as possible. But not Ken. He was in no hurry. He took great delight in sailing his boat. As a true sailor, he received as much enjoyment from sailing as he did from arriving someplace.

Perhaps we feel the same way about our journey to heaven as I did about sailing. Thinking only of how wonderful it will be when we arrive, we grow dissatisfied in the life's trials. We miss out on what God has to offer. As we face challenges, there are truths to be discovered, battles to be won, and spiritual delights to be enjoyed. Let's seek joy in the journey. —DCE

SEPTEMBER 28

The heavens declare the glory of God; the skies proclaim the work of his hands. —Psalm 19:1

When physicist Albert Einstein was asked if he believed in God, he responded, "We are in the position of a little child entering a huge library filled with books in many languages. The child knows someone must have written those books. It does not know how." Although Einstein marveled at the design he saw in nature, he did not believe in a personal Creator.

The psalmist shared Einstein's awe but took the next step—believing in the Designer behind the design: "The heavens declare the glory of God; the skies proclaim the work of his hands" (Psalm 19:1). Are you struggling in your beliefs? Look up at the stars tonight. In the sky is an amazing road sign pointing to the Designer behind the design. —DF

APRIL 5

And if I go and prepare a place for you, I will come back and take you to be with me that you also may be where I am. —John 14:3

Noted nineteenth-century lecturer Wendell Phillips was deeply devoted to his disabled wife. His speaking engagements, however, often required him to be away from her. At the close of a lecture one night in a town several miles from home, Phillips's friends urged him not to attempt the journey until morning. "It's cold and sleeting, and you face several miles of rough riding." His reply was simple. "But at the other end of those miles I shall find my beloved Anne."

As Christians, we can press on because at the end of our journey we will find Jesus. His promise pulls us along: "You also may be where I am" (John 14:3). The road may be rough, the trials many, and the opposition fierce, but we have hope. We will look on the face of our Savior. —PVG

SEPTEMBER 27

I am with you and will watch over you wherever you go. —Genesis 28:15

The highway around the southern shore of Lake Michigan can be treacherous in winter. Once as we were driving back to Michigan from Chicago, snow and ice slowed traffic, caused accidents, and almost doubled our drive time. As we finally reached our home road, my husband said, "Thanks, Lord. I think I can take it from here." Just then, our car spun around 180 degrees. We came to a stop, hearts pounding, almost imagining God saying: "Are you sure?"

Why do we sometimes try to go alone through life when we have access to God every moment? He said: "I am with you and will watch over you wherever you go" (Genesis 28:15). What a comfort to know that God is always with us! —CHK

APRIL 6

The bolts of your gates will be iron and bronze, and your strength will equal your days. —Deuteronomy 33:25

Two weeks into a 12,000-mile bike journey, our twenty-year-old daughter Jane called from Florida. "I'll never make it," she told her older brother Kirk. "You can do it, Jane," he urged. "Don't look at the whole trip. Just take it one day at a time!" She took courage from Kirk's words, and she made it all 12,000 miles.

Do you sometimes wonder if you'll make it as a Christian? The way is long. Temptations are fierce. Your strength is small. The trials are many. Remember God allocates strength in daily amounts. Paul said, "inwardly we are being renewed day by day" (2 Corinthians 4:16). Taking one day at a time is the only way of making it all the way. —DD

SEPTEMBER 26

I have been crucified with Christ and I no longer live, but Christ lives in me. —Galatians 2:20

The saying "Jesus is my copilot" has always troubled me. Whenever I'm in the driver's seat of life, my destination is nowhere good. Jesus is not just a spiritual "copilot" giving occasional directions. He should always be in the driver's seat!

Because Jesus died on the cross, something inside us died too—the power of sin. It's what Paul meant when he said, "I have been crucified with Christ and I no longer live, but Christ lives in me" (Galatians 2:20). With Jesus in the driver's seat, old destinations are off-limits. No more traveling streets of self-centeredness, greed, or lust. No more off-roading into swamps of pride or bitterness. He is at the wheel now! Jesus died so He alone can drive and define us. —JS

APRIL 7

Then Jesus said to his disciples, "Whoever wants to be my disciple must deny themselves and take up their cross and follow me." —Matthew 16:24

This advertisement appeared in a London newspaper in the early 1900s: "Men wanted for hazardous journey. Small wages, bitter cold, long months of complete darkness, constant danger. Safe return doubtful." The ad was placed by Sir Ernest Shackleton, the famous South Pole explorer. The response was overwhelming. This ad reminds me of the words of Christ in Matthew 16:24, "Whoever wants to be my disciple must deny themselves and take up their cross and follow me." Jesus also was looking for those who would go with Him on a hazardous journey—the way of the cross. Thousands have responded to that invitation through the centuries, forsaking all to follow Him. The Lord continues to issue the call for followers. He wants those who are willing to serve Him regardless of the cost. —RD

SEPTEMBER 25

Guard your heart. . . . Give careful thought to the paths for your feet. —Proverbs 4:23, 26

A forty-seven-year-old Austrian gave away his $4.7 million fortune after concluding that wealth and lavish spending were keeping him from real happiness. He told a reporter, "I had the feeling I was working as a slave for things I did not wish for or need. It was the biggest shock in my life when I realized how horrible, soulless, and without feeling the 'five-star' lifestyle is." His money now funds Latin American charities.

Proverbs 4 urges us to consider carefully our own lives. The passage contrasts the free, unhindered path of the just with the dark, confused way of the wicked (v. 19). Who wants to go through life on a heartless road? It can happen, unless we consider exactly where we're going and ask God for direction. —DCM

APRIL 8

Since we are surrounded by such a great cloud of witnesses, let us throw off everything that hinders and the sin that so easily entangles. —Hebrews 12:1

On a warm summer afternoon, three young people and I decided to walk a five-mile stretch along the Tahquamenon River in Michigan's Upper Peninsula. Facing one obstacle after another, we began to slow down. We weren't sure how far we had to go or what lay ahead. Yet we kept pressing on because we knew our friends were waiting at the end of the trail. When we stopped for a rest, we talked about parallels between our walk and the Christian's journey. Highs and lows. Difficulties. Dangers to avoid. When we aren't sure what's ahead and we are discouraged, the temptation is to stop. But the Bible tells us to "run with endurance."

Have you come to a standstill in your Christian life because you are discouraged and tired? If so, I urge you, "Don't stop now!" —DCE

SEPTEMBER 24

*Listen, my sons, to a father's instruction;
pay attention and gain understanding.* —Proverbs 4:1

Native Americans were Michigan's first road engineers. With few exceptions, today's major highways follow trails they cut through the wilderness centuries before white men arrived. In a similar way, Solomon followed the trail of his father, paving the way for his sons and grandsons. He did this by encouraging his sons to heed his instructions just as he had followed the sound teaching of his father, David (Proverbs 4:4–5), who was called a "man after [God's] own heart" (1 Samuel 13:14; Acts 13:22).

Our physical and spiritual children watch the path we're taking. As God's men and women, let's cut a righteous, wise, and clear trail. If ongoing generations choose to follow, the trail can become a highway—an ongoing legacy to God's glory. —DCE

APRIL 9

Therefore, my dear brothers and sisters, stand firm. Let nothing move you. —1 Corinthians 15:58

An article in *Workstyle* magazine emphasized the importance of getting ready for a trip beforehand. It gave guidelines on carrying the right kind and amount of clothing and being prepared for weather variations. The article suggested spending quality time in preparation.

There are some parallels in the Christian's preparation for the time when he goes to heaven. It would be unwise, for example, to wait until the hour of departure to start thinking about the journey. We need to spend quality time preparing for the day we meet the Lord. We do this by investing our life in doing God's will. Concluding his instruction on the resurrection, the apostle Paul advised believers to "give yourselves fully to the work of the Lord" (1 Corinthians 15:58). As we do, we will be packing for heaven. —DCE

SEPTEMBER 23

Be kind and compassionate to one another, forgiving each other, just as in Christ God forgave you.
—Ephesians 4:32

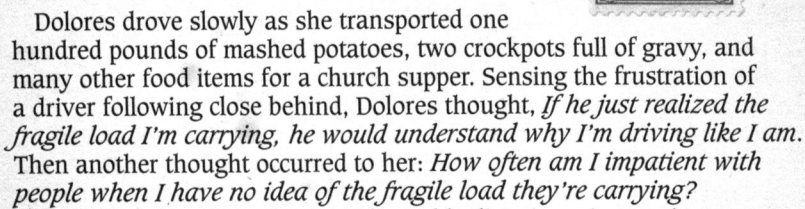

Dolores drove slowly as she transported one hundred pounds of mashed potatoes, two crockpots full of gravy, and many other food items for a church supper. Sensing the frustration of a driver following close behind, Dolores thought, *If he just realized the fragile load I'm carrying, he would understand why I'm driving like I am.* Then another thought occurred to her: *How often am I impatient with people when I have no idea of the fragile load they're carrying?*

God's Word sends us in more charitable directions, instructing us to treat others with kindness, humility, and patience (Colossians 3:12). Let's treat others as we would like to be treated (Luke 6:31), remembering that we don't always know the burden they may be carrying. —CHK

APRIL 10

But whoever does not have them is nearsighted and blind, forgetting that they have been cleansed from their past sins. —2 Peter 1:9

On August 4, 1987, Jim Dickson set sail from Rhode Island for England aboard a 36-foot sloop named *Eye Opener*. What made this so unusual is that Dickson has been legally blind since age seven. The *Eye Opener* was specially equipped for the journey. But several days out at sea, Dickson ran into technical problems. Without reliable equipment, Dickson was forced to abandon his venture.

That story brings to mind our plight as Christians if we try to journey life's seas without adding to our faith the character traits that will carry us through the storms of adversity. They are virtue, knowledge, self-control, perseverance, godliness, brotherly kindness, love (2 Peter 1:5–7). If we cultivate those qualities through prayer and yielding to God's Spirit, we won't be caught sailing blind when life's stormy trials come. —DD

SEPTEMBER 22

God . . . has been my shepherd all my life to this day.
—Genesis 48:15

George Matheson's song "Ignored Blessings" looks back to "the road gone by." By looking back, he could see that his heavenly Father had led him all the way. God has a "course" for each of us to run (Acts 20:24, 2 Timothy 4:7). Our route is rooted in the sovereign purpose of God, yet our choices matter. We make decisions every day, some with life-altering consequences. The question—aside from the confounding mystery of God's sovereignty and human choice—is this: How can we discern our course?

Though clouds surround the present and I don't know the future, my past assures me that the Shepherd will show me the way. My task is to follow Him in love and obedience, trusting each step to Him. —DHR

APRIL 11

Religion that God our Father accepts as pure and faultless is this: to look after orphans and widows in their distress and to keep oneself from being polluted by the world. —James 1:27

A Christian businessman heard his pastor tell about a widow who had been evicted from her home for nonpayment of rent. Her furniture was piled on the lawn. She didn't know where she would go. The pastor said that if someone would help her, he would have a "foretaste of heaven." The businessman went to the home. He returned to church and said, "I have just been in heaven. I went to see that widow, paid her back rent, helped her move her belongings into the house again, and stocked her cupboards with food. It is the most joy I have experienced in years."

Do you want to be in heaven for a little while without leaving earth? Do something kind and unselfish for someone. Follow the example of the businessman, and enjoy a foretaste of heaven. —HVL

SEPTEMBER 21

The LORD your God led you all the way in the wilderness these forty years, to humble and test you. —Deuteronomy 8:2

After writing an *Our Daily Bread* article about obeying the law, I started a long trip determined to drive the speed limit. Before long, I became more occupied with unwrapping a sandwich than watching the signs—and got a speeding ticket. Lesson one was that not paying attention costs the same as deliberate disregard for the law.

Lesson two was that our resolve will always be tested. I recalled Moses' words to the people before entering the Promised Land: "God led you all the way in the wilderness these forty years, to humble and test you in order to know what was in your heart, whether or not you would keep His commands" (Deuteronomy 8:2). God showed me the importance of setting my heart on obedience—and paying attention along the way.
—DCM

APRIL 12

But you will receive power when the Holy Spirit comes on you; and you will be my witnesses in Jerusalem, and in all Judea and Samaria, and to the ends of the earth. —Acts 1:8

The Bible calls us to be witnesses no matter where we live. We need to be genuinely interested in the people next door before we can be interested in those who are far away. This means we must work at maintaining a good testimony. That was undoubtedly true of the first-century Christians. Whether at home in Jerusalem or scattered throughout Judea and Samaria, they gave witness to their faith (Acts 1:8).

Maybe at one time you intended to give your life for overseas service, but plans did not materialize. You can still take up the task—right where you are. Or if you've never felt called to a faraway place, you still live on a mission field. Your part of the world is where Christians are called to go with the gospel. —JP

SEPTEMBER 20

It is written: "Man shall not live on bread alone, but on every word that comes from the mouth of God." —Matthew 4:4

Drive south of our home in Boise, and you'll see a volcanic butte rising out of the sagebrush. This is the initial point from which Idaho was surveyed, beginning in 1867. The survey established the language of land description in the state: Townships are designated north and south of the initial point; ranges are east and west. With such descriptions, you always know exactly where you are.

We may read many books, but the Word of God is our "initial point," the one fixed reference. John Wesley read widely, but always referred to himself as "a man of one book." Nothing can compare to the Word of God. "How sweet are your words to my taste, sweeter than honey to my mouth!" (Psalm 119:103). —DHR

APRIL 13

He makes me lie down in green pastures, he leads me beside quiet waters. —Psalm 23:2

In Exodus 15 we read that the children of Israel experienced the bitterness of Marah. But then God led them on to Elim. What a delightful change they found with its wells of water and its sheltering palms! The people couldn't help but realize that both stops were by God's direction. Both Marah and Elim were marked out by God's cloud that was leading them. Still today, God directs our lives!

Are you now "camped at Marah"? If you're experiencing bitterness, sorrow, or disappointment, keep in mind that you'll soon drink the sweet water of Elim's wells. God's comfort will surely come—both on earth and in heaven. If you're already enjoying the encouragement of Elim, rejoice in it. God is strengthening you for the rest of the journey. —PVG

SEPTEMBER 19

In the morning, LORD, you hear my voice; in the morning I lay my requests before you and wait expectantly. —Psalm 5:3

Teaching my daughters to drive, I added instruction on basic auto maintenance. They learned to check the oil whenever they fueled the car. Adding a quart of oil is nothing compared to replacing an engine.

Maintenance is also important in our spiritual lives. Taking time daily to read the Bible, pray, and listen to God is a key element in avoiding breakdowns. David wrote, "In the morning, LORD, you hear my voice; in the morning I lay my requests before you" (Psalm 5:3). He then poured out his heart in praise, thanksgiving, and requests to God. Many find it essential to begin every day with the Lord. It's not magic—it's maintenance, as we ask Him to fill us with His presence on the road of life. —DCM

APRIL 14

All these people were still living by faith when they died. They did not receive the things promised; they only saw them and welcomed them from a distance. —Hebrews 11:13

When my son was young, we enjoyed discovering that monarch butterflies that spend the summer in Western Michigan don't stick around for cold weather. They go to Mexico. Scientists have discovered several sites where millions upon millions of butterflies from North America spend the winter. Each new generation that migrates has never been there before. Something programmed into their tiny bodies directs them. These butterflies are an example of God's creatures being guided by the mind of their Creator. They also illustrate the children of God referred to in Hebrews 11. These heroes of faith walked roads they had not consciously mapped out, following an inner leading to a land they'd never seen—a land God prepared for them. They remind us that we are pilgrims journeying home. —MD

SEPTEMBER 18

God is our refuge and strength,
an ever-present help in trouble. —Psalm 46:1

    An acquaintance of mine was hunting with friends near Balmoral, country estate of the queen of England. When he twisted his ankle badly, he told his friends to continue while he waited by the roadside. A car came down the road and stopped. The woman inside rolled her window down and offered him a ride. He opened the door to realize it was the queen!

    All of us have an even more astounding offer of help: The Creator-God of the universe descends into our world, sees our trouble, and marshals His resources to help us. He gives us grace to endure, His Word to sustain, and friends to encourage and pray for us. Next time you feel stranded along life's road, look for your Helper. —JS

APRIL 15

My grace is sufficient for you, for my power is made perfect in weakness. —2 Corinthians 12:9

A Christian was explaining to a friend Jesus' sacrifice at Calvary. He said that because of the work of Christ, not a single charge remains against the believer. He then asked, "Isn't that enough?" "No," replied his friend, "that's not enough!" The believer asked, "If you were to fail in business and couldn't pay, what if your creditors forgave all of your debts? Would that be sufficient?" "No," said the other man, "I'd still need cash to live on." The Christian responded: "Jesus gives the believer the Holy Spirit, the Word of God, and full provision for the entire journey to glory."

The apostle Paul knew that the grace of God was sufficient for all his needs. That's why said, "My God will meet all your needs according to the riches of his glory in Christ Jesus" (Philippians 4:19). —PVG

SEPTEMBER 17

Ask for the ancient paths, ask where the good way is, and walk in it, and you will find rest for your souls. —Jeremiah 6:16

Ever heard the saying, "The past is a guidepost, not a hitching post"? It's easy to cling to "the good old days" instead of using our experience as direction for the road ahead. We're all susceptible to the paralysis of nostalgia.

When Jeremiah was called to be a prophet, God said through him, "Stand at the crossroads and look; ask for the ancient paths, ask where the good way is, and walk in it, and you will find rest for your souls" (Jeremiah 6:16). God urged His people to look back so they could move ahead. Considering ancient paths would point to "the good way" marked by God's faithfulness. He teaches from our past that the best road is the one we walk with Him. —DCM

APRIL 16

He stilled the storm to a whisper; the waves of the sea were hushed. They were glad when it grew calm, and he guided them to their desired haven. —Psalm 107:29–30

Edward Hopper pastored a church established for sailors and fishermen. He was intrigued by their accounts of storms and high winds. After preaching one Sunday from Matthew 8, the account of Jesus calming the boisterous Sea of Galilee, he wrote "Jesus, Savior, Pilot Me." The last stanza is beautiful in its simplicity and directness. "When at last I near the shore, / And the fearful breakers roar / 'Twixt me and the peaceful rest— / Then, while leaning on Thy breast, / May I hear Thee say to me, 'Fear not—I will pilot thee!' " Years later, he was composing a song about heaven when he died from a heart attack. He experienced the answer to the prayer expressed years before: "May I hear Thee say to me, / 'Fear not—I will pilot thee.' " When Jesus is at the helm of your life you will arrive safely at the "desired haven" of heaven. —HGB

SEPTEMBER 16

Jesus answered, "It is written: 'Man shall not live on bread alone, but on every word that comes from the mouth of God.'" —Matthew 4:4

During an election in my country, one struggling mom exchanged her vote for a bag of diapers. We had discussed the benefits of each candidate, so her choice disappointed me. "What about your convictions?" I asked. Six months after her candidate won, taxes went even higher. Everything is now more expensive . . . even diapers!

Political corruption is not new. Neither is spiritual corruption. Satan tempted the Lord to "sell" His convictions (Matthew 4:1–10), coming to Jesus when He was tired and hungry. Satan offered immediate satisfaction, but Jesus knew that shortcuts were dangerous enemies. He held firm to what He knew was true from God's Word (vv. 4, 7, 10). When we're tempted, we can depend on God to help us avoid dangerous shortcuts. —KO

APRIL 17

Therefore this is what I will do to you, Israel, and because I will do this to you, Israel, prepare to meet your God. —Amos 4:12

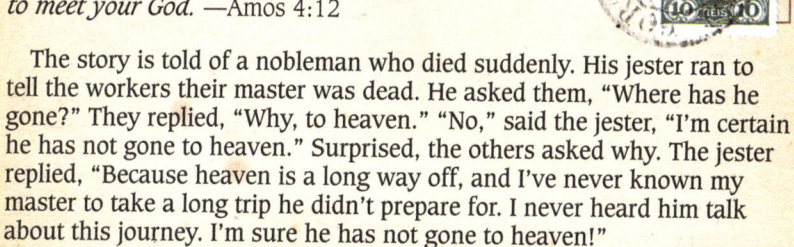

    The story is told of a nobleman who died suddenly. His jester ran to tell the workers their master was dead. He asked them, "Where has he gone?" They replied, "Why, to heaven." "No," said the jester, "I'm certain he has not gone to heaven." Surprised, the others asked why. The jester replied, "Because heaven is a long way off, and I've never known my master to take a long trip he didn't prepare for. I never heard him talk about this journey. I'm sure he has not gone to heaven!"
    We are saved by grace through faith in Christ—not by how much we talk about it. Yet I wonder, would anyone know that you're going to heaven? If you seldom think about it and never discuss it, make sure you are prepared! —RD

SEPTEMBER 15

He lifted me . . . out of the mud and mire; he set my feet on a rock. —Psalm 40:2

We were stuck! While I was laying a wreath on my parents' grave, my husband eased the car off the road to allow another to pass. It had rained for weeks and the area was sodden. When we were ready to leave, the wheels spun, sinking into the mud. We needed help!

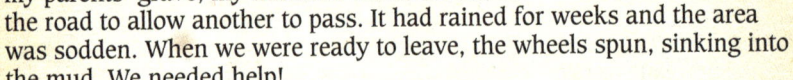

Psalm 40 recounts God's faithfulness when David cried for help. "I waited patiently for the LORD; he turned to me and heard my cry. He lifted me out of the slimy pit, out of the mud and mire" (vv. 1–2). Whether this psalm refers to an actual pit or to challenging circumstances, David knew he could always call on God for deliverance. And God will help us too when we cry. —MS

APRIL 18

My times are in your hands; deliver me from the hands of my enemies, from those who pursue me. —Psalm 31:15

An elderly lady was traveling from Chicago to Bay City, Michigan. She was afraid she was on the wrong train, so she asked the conductor. "Tell me, sir, is this the train to Bay City?" "Yes it is, ma'am," he replied. "Enjoy the trip." And that's what she did. She had the word of authority on it.

We too are on a journey. We travel an unknown pathway, so it's easy to become apprehensive. But like that lady, we can rely on a "word of authority" to quiet our fears—the Bible. With Christ as our Savior and the promises of Scripture in our hearts, we can "enjoy the trip" and travel with unwavering confidence, because we know where we're going! —RD

SEPTEMBER 14

Lord, what do You want me to do? —Acts 9:6 (NKJV)

On June 6, 1944, three American officers huddled in a bombshell crater at Normandy, France. Realizing the tide had carried them to the wrong place on Utah Beach, they made an impromptu decision: "We'll start the battle here."

Likewise, Saul was in a difficult place after meeting Jesus on the road to Damascus (Acts 9:1–20). Suddenly, the arc of his life was revealed as a mistake. Moving forward would be difficult. He might even face the Christian families he'd persecuted. But Saul responded, "Lord, what do You want me to do?" (v. 6).

We often find ourselves in places we never planned. But Scripture says to forget what lies behind and press forward toward Christ (Philippians 3:13–14). The past is no barrier to a better future. —RK

APRIL 19

Seek the LORD while he may be found; call on him while he is near. —Isaiah 55:6

A minister pulled into a busy gas station. A long string of cars lined up, causing quite a delay. When the preacher paid for his gas, the clerk apologized, "I'm sorry. It's like this every holiday. People wait until the last minute—even though they've known about the trip for a while." "I understand," replied the pastor. "I have the same trouble in my business!"

We all know what he was talking about. Many people are aware that someday they'll be going on a journey—one that will take them into eternity. There's no escaping it! But too many wait until the last minute to make preparation for meeting God. That's dangerous, because the date of their passage into eternity is unknown. Sometimes the departure from this life comes years before it's expected. Are you ready for that last great journey? —RD

SEPTEMBER 13

You died, and your life is now hidden with Christ in God. —Colossians 3:3

Two Germans wanted to climb the Matterhorn, so they hired three guides and began the ascent. Roped together, they'd gone only a little way when the last man lost his footing. He was held up by the others, because each had a toehold he'd cut in the ice. Then the next man slipped, pulling down the two above him. The only one to hold was the first guide, who had driven a spike deep into the ice. He was stable, and the others regained their footing.

British minister F. B. Meyer told this story, commenting, "I am like one of those who slipped; but thank God, I am bound in a living partnership to Christ. Because He stands I will never perish." We are safe in Christ. —RD

APRIL 20

Be filled with the Spirit, speaking to one another with psalms, hymns, and songs from the Spirit. Sing and make music from your heart to the Lord. —Ephesians 5:18–19

A driving instructor came up with a new idea. She advised her students to sing or hum quietly to themselves while behind the wheel. The results were amazing. Those who tried it were more relaxed and had fewer accidents.

I'm not saying this technique will automatically work wonders for you. However, I am suggesting that if you are a Christian, you can have peace in your soul even though your earthly pilgrimage seems at times like a frantic freeway journey. Through the indwelling Holy Spirit you can sing and rejoice no matter what is happening around you. The heavenly Father has given you His Spirit, who can fill your life with the joyful songs of redemption. As you travel life's highway today, try the hum-along of "singing and making melody in your heart to the Lord." —PVG

SEPTEMBER 12

We live by faith, not by sight. —2 Corinthians 5:7

A Christian journeying through life is like a hiker on a narrow mountain trail, unable to see the entire path ahead. Sometimes the way is clearly marked; at other times, it turns abruptly, rises or falls, or becomes slippery. All the hiker knows is that he must take the next step. Our spiritual walk differs in some respects. Through faith in Christ, we can move forward with full confidence that we will reach our destination.

Perhaps you are at the rim of a shadowy unknown. Go ahead. Prayerfully step into the future. God has promised to always be there for you (Hebrews 13:5). An anonymous poet said of those steps, "Faith is knowing there'll be something to stand on, or you will be taught to fly."
—DCE

APRIL 21

Because you are my help, I sing in the shadow of your wings. I cling to you; your right hand upholds me.
—Psalm 63:7–8

A family was traveling by car through the mountains at night. The way was unfamiliar and everything was pitch-black except for the lights of the car shining on the road ahead. As one of the little girls peered anxiously through the window, she felt someone place a hand on her shoulder. "Is that you, Daddy?" she said. "Yes, dear," came the reply. Reassured by her father's gentle touch, the youngster leaned back and fell asleep.

This reminds me of the fact that God will never leave us nor forsake us. We can be confident of His nearness in the dark as well as in the light. Right now you may be walking through a deep valley, but you are not alone. Don't be afraid! With the heavenly Father at your side you can say with certainty, "your right hand upholds me." —PVG

SEPTEMBER 11

The folly of fools yields folly. —Proverbs 14:24

    Author Annie Dillard described the provisions the Franklin expedition's ships carried for a hazardous journey across the Arctic Ocean: an auxiliary steam engine, but only a twelve-day supply of coal for the projected two- or three-year voyage; a twelve-hundred-volume library; a hand-organ playing fifty tunes; china place settings for officers and men; and sterling silver flatware. One thing they didn't carry was special clothing for the Arctic. How foolish!

    Some people heading toward eternity are even more shortsighted. Multitudes pay no attention to Jesus' solemn question, "What good will it be for someone to gain the whole world, yet forfeit their soul?" (Matthew 16:26). You can prepare for eternity with total confidence: "Believe in the Lord Jesus, and you will be saved" (Acts 16:31). —VG

APRIL 22

So God led the people around by the desert road toward the Red Sea. The Israelites went up out of Egypt ready for battle. —Exodus 13:18

When the children of Israel left the land of Egypt where they had lived in slavery for more than four centuries, a long period of wandering still lay ahead. The barren experiences of going through the desert must have seemed fruitless and unnecessary to God's chosen people. Certainly the journey would not be pleasant, and they would face many hardships. But these difficulties were needed to help them develop a mature faith and a strong character. Such qualities can never be attained quickly.

Detours take time. The usual route may be faster and seem more desirable, but God knows what is best for us and may direct us to follow another path. If you are taking a detour that seems unproductive and a waste of time, be patient and let God lead you in His appointed way. —PVG

SEPTEMBER 10

The goal of this command is love, which comes from a pure heart and a good conscience and a sincere faith. —1 Timothy 1:5

When you sail, you need to know three important facts: your location, destination, and course. With a map and compass, you can end up where you want to go. I heard about someone who set out to cross Lake Michigan from Milwaukee. Trusting his own sense of direction, he sailed for two hours and spotted a large city on the horizon—Milwaukee! Somehow, he had sailed a huge circle.

So how does a follower of Christ stay on course? Paul mentioned the importance of "a pure heart and a good conscience" (1 Timothy 1:19 NASB). We gain those by carefully reading and following God's Word, depending on the Spirit's leading and help. Determine to live in faith and holiness, staying on course until you're safely home. —DCE

APRIL 23

Do not throw away your confidence; it will be richly rewarded. —Hebrews 10:35

There's an old adage that says, "Don't bite off more than you can chew." This can happen in our walk of faith when our commitment to God seems too much to bear. But Scripture has an encouraging word for us. The writer of Hebrews urged his readers to recall the courage they demonstrated during the early days of their faith (10:32–33). Despite public insults and persecution, they aided believers in prison, and they accepted the confiscation of their property (vv. 33–34). He says, "Do not throw away your confidence . . . . You need to persevere so that when you have done the will of God, you will receive what he has promised" (vv. 35–36).

God's power enables us to go on. Recalling the Lord's faithfulness in days past stirs our confidence in Him today. —DCM

SEPTEMBER 9

Have the same mindset as Christ Jesus: Who, being in very nature God, did not consider equality with God something to be used to his own advantage; rather, he made himself nothing by taking the very nature of a servant. —Philippians 2:5–7

In his book *First Man*, James Hansen chronicles Neil Armstrong's flight to the moon. The author explains how each astronaut filled out a report upon completion of the flight, listing their travels from Houston to Cape Canaveral, the moon, the Pacific Ocean, Hawaii, and then back to Houston. What a list of destinations! There is another itinerary that outshines any trip ever taken. Imagine this travel guide of our Savior, Jesus Christ: Place of origin—heavenly places; Initial destination—Bethlehem; Mode of travel—virgin birth; Reason for travel—redemption of sinners; Return destination—right hand of the Father. His extraordinary itinerary should fill our hearts with gratitude and praise! —DF

APRIL 24

The LORD is my rock, my fortress and my deliverer; my God is my rock, in whom I take refuge, my shield and the horn of my salvation. —2 Samuel 22:2–3

In the Kofa Mountains, the only palms native to Arizona jut from the red granite sides of a canyon. These tropical plants flourish and remain strong on the dark, almost perpendicular sides of this narrow gorge, yet the sun reaches them only two hours a day. Botanists were puzzled until they concluded that the stone walls must reflect enough light and store enough warmth to enable these trees to thrive in the cold shadows of the canyon.

In these palms we see a parable. Believers who live in close fellowship with God can endure any difficulty. Why? Because the Rock on which they stand provides the love and comfort they need to thrive. Founded on God—the Rock of their strength and salvation—redeemed souls can remain joyful and productive even in the darkest circumstances. —HGB

SEPTEMBER 8

Your word is a lamp for my feet, a light on my path.
—Psalm 119:105

God usually doesn't show where He's taking us. He just asks us to trust Him. It's like driving a car at night. Our headlights never shine all the way to our destination; they illuminate about 160 feet ahead.

God's Word is like headlights in dark times. It is full of promises we need to keep us from driving into the ditch of despair. His Word promises He will never leave us nor forsake us (Hebrews 13:5), assures us that He has plans to give us "hope and a future" (Jeremiah 29:11), and tells us our trials arise to make us better, not bitter (James 1:2–4).

Next time you feel like you're driving through darkness, remember to trust your "headlights." God's Word will light your way. —JS

APRIL 25

In all your ways submit to him, and he will make your paths straight. —Proverbs 3:6

"Don't worry. I know right where I'm going," I said to my passengers. Then an almost-human voice ratted me out: "Rerouting . . . rerouting." Now everyone knew I was lost! I was told on by my GPS.

Sometimes followers of Jesus need help in getting back on track spiritually after failing to notice we're moving further and further from the walk God wants with us. God has not left us on our own, however. He has given all believers the Holy Spirit (John 14:16–17; 1 Corinthians 3:16), who convicts us of our sin (John 16:8,13). When we're going off course, He sounds the alarm and triggers our conscience (Galatians 5:16–25). What comfort to know that God is at work in our lives through the convicting work of the Holy Spirit! (Romans 8:26–27). —RK

SEPTEMBER 7

I am torn between the two: I desire to depart and be with Christ, which is better by far.
—Philippians 1:23

We who know Jesus have an incredible destination ahead. But a lot of us don't seem excited about getting to heaven. Why? Maybe we don't understand heaven. We talk about streets of gold, but what can we look forward to, really?

A profound description of heaven comes from Paul, who said that to "depart and be with Christ" is "better by far" (Philippians 1:23). When my eight-year-old grandson asked what heaven is like, I asked him, "What is the most exciting thing in your life?" He mentioned some things he enjoys. When I told him heaven is far better, he thought for a minute and said, "Papa, that's hard to imagine." What excites you? Whatever it is, although it's hard to imagine, heaven will be far better! —JS

APRIL 26

Where, O death, is your victory? Where, O death, is your sting? —1 Corinthians 15:55

I've heard people say, "I'm not afraid of death because I'm confident I'm going to heaven; it's the dying process that scares me!" As Christians, we look forward to heaven but we may be afraid of dying. Why don't Christians need to fear death? Because Jesus was raised from the grave, and we who are in Christ will also be raised. That's why Paul proclaimed: "The sting of death is sin . . . . But thanks be to God! He gives us the victory through our Lord Jesus Christ" (1 Corinthians 15:56–57).

The dying process is an escort that ushers us into eternity with God. As we "walk through the valley of the shadow of death," we can have this confidence: "You are with me; Your rod and Your staff, they comfort me" (Psalm 23:4 NKJV). —AL

SEPTEMBER 6

The ways of the LORD are right; the righteous walk in them. —Hosea 14:9

Asking directions is not my favorite thing. My wife, on the other hand, is eager to seek guidance. In the end, she's the wiser one, getting to her destination quickly and without angst. I get lost.

Thinking we're smart enough to navigate life on our own goes against a warning of Scripture: "There is a way that appears to be right, but in the end it leads to death" (Proverbs 16:25). When we're at a fork in the road, we should stop and consult God, because "the ways of the LORD are right" (Hosea 14:9). Asking Him for directions isn't just a good idea—it's critical. "Trust in the LORD with all your heart . . . he will make your paths straight" (Proverbs 3:5–6). —JS

APRIL 27

Jesus went through all the towns and villages, teaching in their synagogues, proclaiming the good news of the kingdom. —Matthew 9:35

A pastor in Nepal told me of a trip of about a hundred miles he was planning to take on a motorcycle to preach. But it turned out a bit differently from what he envisioned. "We had a wonderful time of marching in the mountains with our church members," he told me later. "All do not have motorcycles . . . so we all walked. It was a blessed time." I was reminded of how "Jesus went through all the towns and villages, . . . proclaiming the good news of the kingdom" (Matthew 9:35).

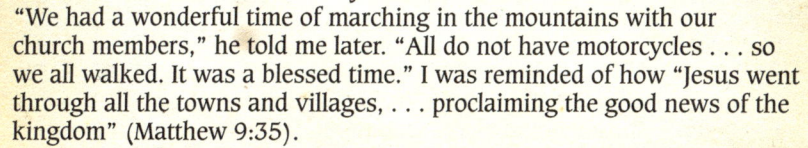

I thought of my reluctance to drive across town in the snow to visit a lonely widower or to walk across the street to help a neighbor. And I thought of our Lord, for whom no distance was too great. —DHR

SEPTEMBER 5

[Apollos] was a great help to those who by grace had believed. —Acts 18:27

Geese fly at speeds of 40 to 50 miles per hour, traveling in formation because, as each bird flaps its wings, an updraft is created for the bird behind it. They can go 70 percent farther in a group than if they flew alone.

In a way, followers of Christ are like that. As we work together, moving toward a common goal, we strengthen and help one another (Acts 18:23, 27). We can accomplish more together than we can by ourselves. And geese honk to encourage each other. Those in the rear sound off to exhort those up front to stay on course and maintain their speed. Is there anyone flying in formation with you today to whom you might give some "helpful honks"? —HR

APRIL 28

You will know that it was the LORD who brought you out of Egypt. —Exodus 16:6

    The first time I saw her, I fell in love. She was a beauty. Sleek. Radiant. As soon as I spied the 1962 Thunderbird, her shiny exterior and killer interior beckoned me. I plunked down eight hundred dollars and purchased my first car. But there was a problem lurking inside. A few months after I bought my T-Bird, it suddenly couldn't go backward. It had no reverse. Sometimes it's good for us to be like my old car. We need to keep going forward. Paul said it simply: We need to "press on toward the goal" (Philippians 3:14). Perhaps the children of Israel could have used my T-Bird's transmission. Despite the many miracles God had performed, they kept looking back at Egypt.

    Keep moving ahead in your walk with God. Don't back up. Press on.
—DB

SEPTEMBER 4

At the sight of these people Paul thanked God and was encouraged. —Acts 28:15

Several friends were scaling Mt. Rainier. When they reached a plateau, most decided they'd gone far enough. But a man named Ragnar continued climbing to find a friend who'd traveled ahead. Eventually Ragnar found him resting, enjoying the scenery. The man was ready to go back, but when he saw his friend approaching, exclaimed, "Since you've come, let's go higher!"

I'm reminded of the apostle Paul, traveling to Rome. When he met fellow believers at a place called Three Taverns, "at the sight of these people Paul thanked God and was encouraged" (Acts 28:15). What better compliment could we hear than, "Talking to you has encouraged me to continue on my spiritual walk." May we influence others in such a way that they say, "I want to go higher!" —RD

APRIL 29

"Come," he replied, "and you will see." —John 1:39

In many stores, employees take customers to find what they are looking for rather than simply giving them directions. This act of walking alongside an inquiring person may help us expand our concept of what it means to lead others to Christ. When two curious disciples of John the Baptist asked Jesus where He was staying, the Lord said, "Come and see" (John 1:39 NKJV).

Witnessing for Christ may involve walking alongside people who are seeking help and wholeness. Our interest in their spiritual welfare, our prayers, and our involvement with them says without words, "Come and see. Let's walk together, and I'll take you to Him." —DCM

SEPTEMBER 3

Teach me your way, LORD; lead me in a straight path.
—Psalm 27:11

A teenager decided to take a different way to work. On an unfamiliar city street, he went through an intersection without seeing a stop sign. Within seconds, he was stopped. A police officer pulled the boy over and reminded him to observe traffic signs. It cost the teen eighty dollars to learn about that road.

What if he'd had a guide, someone to tell him which way to go and what dangers lay ahead? In life, we often must travel unfamiliar paths, and to do that without making costly mistakes, we need Someone who knows the way. "Lead me, LORD, in your righteousness," the psalm writer said. "Make your way straight before me" (Psalm 5:8).

Is your path unfamiliar? Ask your Father to travel with you. —DB

APRIL 30

Simon Peter answered Him, "Lord, to whom shall we go? You have the words of eternal life." —John 6:68

One of my toughest experiences as a pastor was telling a member of our church that her husband, her son, and her father-in-law had all drowned in a boating accident. There was deep brokenness, haunting doubt, and confusion in her life. But she clung to Jesus. Rather than deserting Him in the midst of her desperation, she ran to Him as the only source of hope and confidence.

In John 6, some of Jesus' followers deserted Him. The Lord turned to His inner circle, and asked, "You do not want to leave too, do you?" (v. 67). Peter responded, "Lord, to whom shall we go? You have the words of eternal life" (v. 68). Whatever you face today, be encouraged by the words of Peter. Run in the right direction—to Jesus—and you'll find the grace and strength you need. —JS

SEPTEMBER 2

*See, your king comes to you, gentle and
riding on a donkey, and on a colt, the foal of a donkey.*
—Matthew 21:5

A minister described Christ's triumphal entry into Jerusalem and asked: "What if the donkey on which Jesus rode thought all the cheering was for him?" The minister then pointed to himself and said, "I'm a donkey. The longer I'm here the more you'll realize that. I am only a Christ-bearer and not the object of praise." On Palm Sunday, the donkey was merely a Christ-bearer, bringing the Son of God into the city where He would give His life for the sins of the world.

If we could develop a healthy "donkey mentality," what an asset that would be as we travel the road of life! Instead of wondering what people think of us, our concern would be, "Can they see Jesus, the King?"
—DCM

MAY 1

The earth is full of his unfailing love.
—Psalm 33:5

On a frigid November day, I was grumbling to myself as I raked and bagged the last of my leaves. Then a cheery voice said, "Good morning!" The woman who reads our gas meter had walked up unnoticed. I asked, "How are you on this blustery morning?" With a smile, she said, "Richly blessed." After a quick attitude adjustment, I replied, "So am I. Isn't God wonderful?" "He sure is," she answered. "Are you a believer in Jesus too?" "Yes, I am," I responded, "and He has filled my life with blessing." That brief exchange not only brightened my mood, but it also reminded me that we who believe in Christ are blessed beyond measure.

Let's encourage one another. We never know when a fellow pilgrim may need a reminder of the goodness of God. —DCE

SEPTEMBER 1

By day the LORD went ahead of them in a pillar of cloud to guide them on their way. —Exodus 13:21

The pillar of cloud was provided to guide the Israelites. So too the Holy Spirit leads the Christian. "When he, the Spirit of truth, comes," Jesus said, "he will guide you into all the truth" (John 16:13). Just as the cloud remained with Israel in the wilderness, Jesus promised that the Spirit would "be with" believers forever (John 14:16). Think of it! God himself dwells within our hearts. We who know Jesus Christ as Savior and Lord are temples of His Holy Spirit (1 Corinthians 6:19).

When we are led by the Spirit, our lives are characterized by love, joy, peace, and self-control (Galatians 5:16, 22–23). We will be effective witnesses for Christ as we travel through the wilderness of this world. —RD

MAY 2

I pray that out of his glorious riches he may strengthen you with power through his Spirit in your inner being. —Ephesians 3:16

Dana and Rich went out for a bike ride expecting to come home refreshed. Instead, Rich lost control of his bike and crashed. His body was mangled, and he barely made it to the hospital alive. Dana faithfully kept vigil by her husband's side. He couldn't feed himself, and he couldn't walk. One day, as they sat under a shade tree outside the hospital, Rich said, "Dana, I don't know if I'll ever walk again, but I'm learning to walk closer to Jesus, and that's what I really want."

In the midst of our trials, we need to think about someone like Rich to help us adjust our perspective—to remind us of the remarkable relationship we have with God through Jesus Christ. As Rich found out, walking with Jesus doesn't depend on our legs. It depends on our heart. —DB

AUGUST 31

He wanted to justify himself, so he asked Jesus, "And who is my neighbor?" —Luke 10:29

In the movie *The Four Feathers*, an Englishman is lost in the vast African desert. Nearing death, he is rescued by Abou Fatma, who shows him great kindness. The Englishman asks why. Fatma's response: "God put you in my way!"

In Jesus' parable of the good Samaritan, a priest and a religious scholar, whose calling was to help people, ignored the needs of a traveler who'd been robbed and left to die. A hated Samaritan, however, gave his time and resources "and took care of him" (Luke 10:34). The ravaged man had been put in the way of three people, but only the Samaritan responded.

In life, we are challenged to meet others' needs. How will we respond to those God puts in our way? —BC

MAY 3

[He] was glad and encouraged them all to remain true to the Lord with all their hearts. —Acts 11:23

When Jean was a teenager, she often walked through a park where mothers sat on benches talking. Their toddlers sat on the swings, wanting a push. "When you push a kid on a swing, which I did," says Jean, "pretty soon he's pumping, doing it himself. That's my role in life—to give others a push."

Encouraging others is a worthy purpose. Barnabas, a godly man mentioned in the book of Acts, had that gift. In the days of the early church, he sold some land and gave the money to the church to use for the less fortunate (4:36–37). When the Jerusalem church heard that people in Antioch were trusting Jesus, they sent Barnabas because he "encouraged them all" (11:23). We too can give others a "push" of encouragement in their walk with the Lord. —AC

AUGUST 30

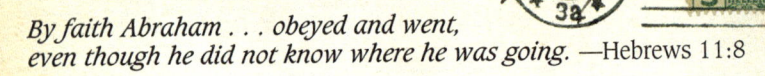

By faith Abraham . . . obeyed and went,
even though he did not know where he was going. —Hebrews 11:8

When Abraham was seventy-five years old, God called him to leave his father's land. Advanced in years, he "did not know where he was going" (Hebrews 11:8)—but he obeyed. Age brings change, the transition from a familiar past to an uncertain future. It can include movement from a family home to a smaller place, a daughter's home, a retirement village, or a nursing home. But we can be at home anywhere, for our safekeeping lies not in a place but in God himself. We can dwell "in the shelter of the Most High" and "rest in the shadow of the Almighty" (Psalm 91:1).

Though our dwelling place here may be uncertain, God will be our companion until we reach our heart's true home. —DHR

MAY 4

Walk in the way of love, just as Christ loved us. —Ephesians 5:2

Our house in Boise, Idaho, backs up to a park with a walking track. You can see most of the path from our kitchen window, and because of that I've learned to recognize people by their walk. There's a lawyer from down the street who's always in a hurry, an elderly man who trudges slowly by, a woman who strides with purposeful steps. Each has a characteristic gait.

What do others see as I walk by? The Bible instructs us: "Walk in the way of love, just as Christ loved us" (Ephesians 5:2) and "Be wise in the way you act" (Colossians 4:5). I ask myself, "Does my walk reflect God's love and wisdom?" Is your life making a difference in the lives around you? Do others see Jesus in what you say and do? —DHR

AUGUST 29

All the earth bows down to you; they sing praise to you.
—Psalm 66:4

"Keep on travelin'. Keep on . . ." The teenage chorale had just started a Sunday evening concert when everything went dark. All power was gone. Well, not the true power. The students kept singing. Midway through the concert, the director asked the congregation to sing along. God's name was lifted high in that darkened church. Beforehand, someone had made sure all the electrical equipment was working. When the power went out, God's power was highlighted. His light, not electric light, shone through.

Sometimes our plans break down, our efforts fall short. When we can't control what happens, we must "keep on travelin' "—remembering where the real power for godly living and praise comes from. Keep lifting up Jesus. It's all about Him anyway. —DB

MAY 5

On the seventh day [God] rested from all His work.
—Genesis 2:2

Answer these questions to determine if you need to rest: Do I feel stressed when functioning in my normal day-to-day activities? Is it difficult to find joy? Do I get the kind of rest my body needs? Do I wake up tired? In creation, God established a pattern of work and rest—a model for believers. For six days God worked to bring order to our world. On the seventh day, after He had finished all His creative activity, He rested.

Jesus showed us the importance of rest when He sat wearily beside a well after a long walk (John 4:6). If the Lord rested from the work of creation and from His earthly ministry, we need to rest from our work as well. Rest refreshes us for service. Schedule some "slow down" time this week. —MW

AUGUST 28

Jesus answered, "I am the way and the truth and the life. No one comes to the Father except through me." —John 14:6

The Roman Empire was known for wide, heavily traveled highways. Jesus' audience would have pictured them when He claimed, "I am the way" (John 14:6). Jesus is the way to heaven, and more. He is our trail-guide who makes new ways for us to live. While the world loves friends and hates enemies, Jesus carves out a new way: "Love your enemies and pray for those who persecute you" (Matthew 5:44). It's easy to judge others, but Jesus says remove the plank from your own eye first (7:3–4). He cuts a path to generous instead of selfish living (Luke 12:13–34).

When Jesus said "I am the way," He called us to leave the old ways that lead to destruction, following Him in His new ways of life. —JS

MAY 6

When he, the Spirit of truth, comes, he will guide you into all the truth. He will not speak on his own; he will speak only what he hears, and he will tell you what is yet to come. —John 16:13

A trip to London—on which I took a guided tour—taught me that there is something new to learn in every setting, especially if we have a guide. Years ago a friend encouraged me to read the entire Bible through every year. Each time I've done it, the Spirit has shown me new things in familiar passages.

Jesus said of the Spirit of truth: "He will guide you into all the truth. He will not speak on his own; he will speak only what he hears, and He will tell you what is yet to come" (John 16:13). It's exciting to anticipate what we will learn from the Bible every day. As we read each page, the Holy Spirit longs to show us something new to meet our needs. Expect an enlightening guided tour. —DCM

AUGUST 27

I will very gladly spend for you everything I have and expend myself as well.
—2 Corinthians 12:15

    Before my husband and I travel, we go to the bank and trade our US dollars for the currency of the country we'll be visiting. We do this so we can pay for expenses while we're away from home. When we become Christians, another kind of exchange takes place. Our lives are like currency that we convert from one medium to another. We trade our old life for a new one so we can begin "spending" ourselves in a different kingdom. Instead of spending ourselves for the causes of this world, we are able to start spending ourselves for the cause of Christ.
    Conversion is far more than just changing our final destination. It's changing the way we spend each day of our lives. —JAL

MAY 7

*I broke the bars of your yoke and enabled
you to walk with heads held high.* —Leviticus 26:13

After four hundred years of slavery, the people of Israel were burdened and discouraged. But under Moses, God led them out bondage. He said, "I am the LORD your God, who brought you out of Egypt so that you would no longer be slaves to the Egyptians; I . . . enabled you to walk with heads held high" (Leviticus 26:13).

This is a vivid reminder of what God has done for us through Jesus Christ. Paul wrote: "Stand firm, then, and do not let yourselves be burdened again by a yoke of slavery" (Galatians 5:1). We don't need to be bowed down with our sin. As we embrace the freedom of righteousness through faith in Jesus, we can hold our heads high and walk tall. —DCM

AUGUST 26

*Anyone who hates a brother or sister . . .
[does] not know where they are going.* —1 John 2:11

GPS is everywhere, but my husband and I still navigate with maps. Since Jay usually drives, the map-watching role is mine. I'm not so good trying to navigate in a moving car. I can't decide the best way to get there if we don't first stop to find out where we are.

That's also true in our spiritual lives. To determine the way God wants us to go, we should first stop and get our spiritual bearings. In helping His disciples navigate life, Jesus often said "stop": "Stop grumbling," "stop judging by mere appearances," "stop doubting and believe" (John 6:43; 7:24; 20:27). To follow Jesus, we frequently have to stop something we're doing wrong. Then we can learn the way He says is right. —JAL

MAY 8

Those who hope in the LORD will renew their strength.
They will soar on wings like eagles. —Isaiah 40:31

   Isaiah's words about patiently waiting for the Lord anticipate the future with confident hope. Knowing that our destiny is glorious, which is the sure hope of heaven, we're able to pick up our pace here on earth. Though weary, we can stretch the wings of our faith! A better world is coming, when our spirits will call us to action and our bodies will run and leap and fly! This is our hope.

   In the meantime, what will be true one day can begin to be true now. We can be steadfast, patient, and joyful in spite of deep weariness; less focused on our frailty and fatigue; more concerned about others than about ourselves; ready to speak a loving word to those who are struggling. We can get ready now for the day our souls will take flight. —DHR

AUGUST 25

Our citizenship is in heaven. —Philippians 3:20

A friend and I took an afternoon horse ride. We slowly roamed through wildflower fields and wooded groves. But when we nosed the animals back toward the barn, they took off for home like rockets. Our horses knew it was time for dinner and a good brushing—and they could hardly wait.

As Christians, we enjoy God's gifts—marriage, children, travel, friends. But we should also focus on "things above" (Colossians 3:1–2): God's enduring presence (Revelation 22:3–5), unending rest (Hebrews 4:9), and an everlasting inheritance (1 Peter 1:4). If we put our faith in God, He'll give us a desire for His heavenly country, loosening our grip on this fallen world. —JBS

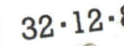

MAY 9

Jesus replied, "No one who puts a hand to the plow and looks back is fit for service in the kingdom of God." —Luke 9:62

Dr. M. R. DeHaan used to tell the story of how his uncle taught him to plow. He said, "He would make a 'back furrow' in the middle of the field. If this row was straight, all the others would fall in line. Finally the time came for me to try my hand. I had often seen him go across the field as straight as an arrow. So I asked him the secret of his success. He replied, 'Just look straight ahead.' Then, giving me the reins, he said, 'I'll stand at the other end, and you keep your eye on me.' " That is also the secret of the victorious Christian life: keep looking to Jesus.

Follow the Lord no matter what it costs, Christian. Never waver, but by His grace go on "plowing a straight furrow." —HGB

AUGUST 24

Take the child and his mother and escape to Egypt. —Matthew 2:13

Traveling through Ohio on the way to Grandma's house, we arrived in Columbus just as a tornado warning was issued. Everything changed as we feared our children might be in danger. That may help us imagine what it was like for Joseph, as he, Mary, and young Jesus traveled to Egypt. Not a tornado but King Herod threatened them. Imagine their fear, knowing that "Herod is going to search for the child to kill him" (Matthew 2:13).

Imagining Jesus' family in danger should give us a feeling of awe regarding the incarnation. Jesus, who enjoyed the majesty of heaven with the Father, set it all aside to be born in poverty, face many dangers, and be crucified for us. Leaving for Egypt is one thing, but leaving heaven for us—that's amazing! —DB

MAY 10

The Word became flesh and made his dwelling among us. We have seen his glory. —John 1:14

After the Apollo 15 moon mission in 1971, Colonel James Irwin spoke of the impact the experience had on his spiritual life. Irwin said that if we think it a great event to go to the moon, how much greater is the wonder that God came to earth in the person of Jesus Christ!

Because man walked on the moon, science and technology have made tremendous advances. But because God walked on earth, we know both our origin and our destiny. We can know our Creator personally (John 1:1, 14, 18), and we can live in His light (v. 9). Through Jesus' sinless life and sacrificial death, we can know the joy of having our sins forgiven and experience the fullness of an abundant life—all because God walked on the earth. —MD

AUGUST 23

*When he, the Spirit of truth, comes,
he will guide you into all the truth.* —John 16:13

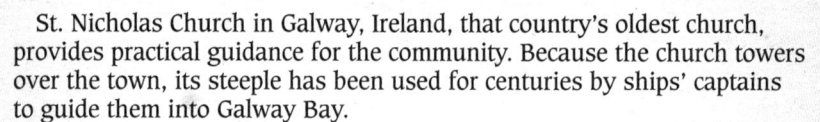

St. Nicholas Church in Galway, Ireland, that country's oldest church, provides practical guidance for the community. Because the church towers over the town, its steeple has been used for centuries by ships' captains to guide them into Galway Bay.

It's not just sailors who need guidance. Jesus addressed this need during His Upper Room Discourse. He said that after His departure the Holy Spirit would play a crucial role in the lives of believers. Jesus promised, "When he, the Spirit of truth, comes, he will guide you into all the truth" (John 16:13). In a world of confusion and fear, we need guidance. God's Spirit is here to help, direct, and guide. Set your course by the "Spirit of truth," and you'll reach safe harbor. —BC

MAY 11

I consider my life worth nothing to me; my only aim is to finish the race and complete the task the Lord Jesus has given me. —Acts 20:24

Former president of Columbia International University Robertson McQuilkin expressed his desire to remain faithful to the Lord with this prayer: "Lord, let me get home before dark." He explained this by saying, "I fear . . . that I should end before I finish, or finish but not well. That I should stain Your honor, shame Your name, grieve Your loving heart. Few, they tell me, finish well."

McQuilkin's words echo the longing of the apostle Paul as he faced danger in Jerusalem: "My only aim is to finish the race and complete the task the Lord Jesus has given me—the task of testifying to the good news of God's grace" (Acts 20:24). Let's keep walking and trusting as we pray, "By Your grace, Father, I humbly ask you to help me get home before dark." —DCM

AUGUST 22

We are hard pressed on every side, but not crushed.
—2 Corinthians 4:8

    Sailboats have lead weights in their keels, providing ballast to keep them upright in strong winds. It's a lot like that in the Christian's life. Our power to survive challenges resides not in us but with God, who dwells within us. We're not exempt from the storms that inevitably threaten our stability. But with full confidence in His power to sustain us, we can say with Paul, "We are hard pressed on every side, but not crushed; perplexed, but not in despair; persecuted, but not abandoned; struck down, but not destroyed" (2 Corinthians 4:8–9).

    Embrace with unshakable confidence the truth that God's grace is sufficient—that in our weakness He is made strong (2 Corinthians 12:9). It will be ballast to your soul. —JS

MAY 12

Everyone who calls on the name of the Lord will be saved. —Romans 10:13

During Canada's pioneer days, a man named Victor and his guide traveled from Fort Babine to the nearest town for supplies. On the way back, snow and poor visibility stopped them. They built a fire and waited out the frigid night. The next morning they awoke to a surprise—they were just yards from the warmth of the fort!

The Israelites were at the border of the Promised Land (Numbers 13). Caleb and Joshua encouraged the people to take possession of the land (vv. 26, 30). But the people doubted, condemning themselves to forty years of wandering and death in the desert (14:28–30). They were so near yet so far away! Have you heard about Jesus' love for you—but remain uncommitted to Him? Choose now to cross over into the "promised land" of salvation found in Jesus. —VG

AUGUST 21

I do not run like someone running aimlessly.
—1 Corinthians 9:26

A rolling-ball clock in the British Museum illustrates the deadening effects of routine. A small steel ball travels in grooves across a tilted steel plate until it trips a lever on the other side. The plate then tilts back, reversing the direction of the ball and advancing the clock hands. Every year, the steel ball travels some 2,500 miles back and forth, but never really goes anywhere.

Routine becomes lethal when we can't see a purpose in it. The apostle Paul overcame his routines—travel, teaching, even confinement—because he believed he could serve Christ his Lord in every situation. Paul committed to cross the finish line in the race of faith and found meaning even in the routine of everyday experience. So can we. —DCM

MAY 13

[Jesus] said: "Whoever wants to be my disciple must deny themselves and take up their cross and follow me." —Mark 8:34

During World War II, B-17 bombers made long flights from the US mainland to the Pacific island of Saipan. When they landed, the planes were met by a jeep bearing the sign: "Follow Me!" That little vehicle guided the giant planes to their assigned parking places. One pilot, who admitted he was not a religious man, made an insightful comment: "That little jeep with its quaint sign always reminds me of Jesus. He was [a lowly] peasant, but the giant men and women of our time would be lost without His direction."

How do we follow Jesus' ways? We turn from our sin and entrust our lives to Him as our Savior. Then, we seek His will in His Word. If you want to get in line with God's purposes, respond to Jesus' invitation: "Follow Me!" —VG

AUGUST 20

Your word is a lamp for my feet,
a light on my path. —Psalm 119:105

During World War II, small compasses protected twenty-seven sailors three hundred miles off the North Carolina coast. A German submarine fired on the SS *Alcoa Guide*, causing the ship to catch fire and begin sinking. The crew escaped in compass-equipped lifeboats, using the directional devices to guide them toward shipping lanes where they were rescued days later.

A psalm writer reminds us that God's Word is a trustworthy compass, likened to a lamp. In ancient times, the flickering light of an olive oil lamp was only enough to show a traveler his next step. But it illuminated the path for those pursuing God (Psalm 119:105). When we lose our bearings in life, God's trustworthy Word is our compass, leading us into deeper fellowship with Him. —MW

MAY 14

I have come that they may have life, and have it to the full. —John 10:10

    A veteran mountain climber was sharing his experiences with a group of novices preparing for their first major climb. "Remember this," he said, "your goal is to experience the exhilaration of the climb and the joy of reaching . . . the peak. If your purpose for climbing is just to avoid death, your experience will be minimal." I see an application to the Christian's experience. Our purpose in following Christ should not be merely to avoid eternal punishment. If that's our primary motivation, we are missing the wonders and joys and victories of climbing higher and higher with Jesus. The Lord promised us "life . . . to the full" (John 10:10). We cannot experience a full and abundant life if we are living in fear.

    Do not live minimally. Live life to the maximum! Climb that mountain with confidence! —DCE

AUGUST 19

They arrived at Ephesus, where Paul left Priscilla and Aquila. He himself went into the synagogue and reasoned with the Jews.
—Acts 18:19

    Are you discouraged because a work God called you to do is starting slowly? Some of our greatest inventions started the same way. The first electric light was so dim a candle was needed to see its socket. The Wright brothers' first airplane flew only twelve seconds. Early automobiles crept along and broke down; people in passing carriages shouted, "Get a horse!" But look what these inventions do today.

    Every Sabbath, the apostle Paul visited the Corinth synagogue, trying to persuade Jews that Jesus is the Christ. They refused his message, so he turned to the Gentiles. Many of them believed and eventually a church was established. What began with little promise ultimately prospered. Don't let rough beginnings get you down. Stick with God's calling! —DCE

MAY 15

Yea, though I walk through the valley of the shadow of death, I will fear no evil; for You are with me.
—Psalm 23:4 (NKJV)

Author William H. Ridgeway recalls that when he was a boy he and his friends would wait on the east side of a railroad track. As the sun sank in the west, a train would come by and "run over them." Of course it didn't actually run over them—just the shadow passed over them. As the train swept by, they were in its shadow for just a few moments. Then it was gone. The setting sun bathed them in a golden glow as they walked to the inviting warmth of home. Can this be a picture of what it means for the Christian to "walk through the valley of the shadow of death"? (Psalm 23:4 NKJV).

We need not fear the chilling shadow of death. We have a home with Him waiting for us just beyond (2 Corinthians 5:1–8). —HGB

AUGUST 18

[He] was caught up to paradise and heard inexpressible things. —2 Corinthians 12:4

After my friend Gus, a fellow trout fisherman, passed away, I got a letter from his daughter Heidi. She's been talking about heaven with her grandkids since Gus went there. Her six-year-old grandson explained what heaven is like and what Great-Grandpa Gus is doing: "It's really beautiful, and Jesus is showing Grandpa Gus where the best fishing holes are."

When Paul reported his God-given vision of heaven, words failed him. He said he "heard things so astounding that they cannot be expressed in words" (2 Corinthians 12:4 NLT). Our words cannot convey heaven's wonders. That's okay, because it's not the knowledge of heaven that assures us. It is our knowledge of God himself. Because I know Him and how good He is, I can leave this life with confidence. Jesus is there, and He'll show me "where the best fishing holes are." That's the kind of God He is! —DHR

MAY 16

You will shine among them like stars in the sky as you hold firmly to the word of life.
—Philippians 2:15–16

In 1982, a London pastor, spurred by the witness of a man outside his church steps, invited members of his church to join him in street evangelism. After a time of training and prayer, they walked the sidewalks near the church every Saturday morning, talking with people about Jesus.

Our churches are to be places of friendship and support. But perhaps, like the pastor in London, we need to raise our eyes to see people just beyond the walls of our traditional practice. It's important to share the glow of worship together, but the sidewalks of life are filled with people who need to see the light of Christ shining through us (Philippians 2:15). Let's step outside and shine "like stars in the sky." —DCM

AUGUST 17

*I am torn between the two: I desire to depart
and be with Christ, which is better by far.* —Philippians 1:23

On the day Sue and I moved to a new home after 26 years in our first home, we did a walk-through to relive the memories. The toughest moment came when we entered Melissa's bedroom. We had said goodbye to her two years earlier after a car accident took her earthly life at age 17. Now we were bidding adieu to the sunflower-themed room she loved so much. As I recall that time, I'm reminded of the great change of address Melissa enjoyed on the day she was ushered into God's presence. Our move to a different house pales in comparison to the glories our daughter enjoys in heaven. What a grand comfort to know that our departed loved ones who have trusted Jesus now live in God's majestic kingdom! (2 Corinthians 5:1).

Are you ready for that ultimate change of address? No matter where you live on this earth, make sure your final home will be heaven. —DB

MAY 17

*The eternal God is your refuge, and
underneath are the everlasting arms.* —Deuteronomy 33:27

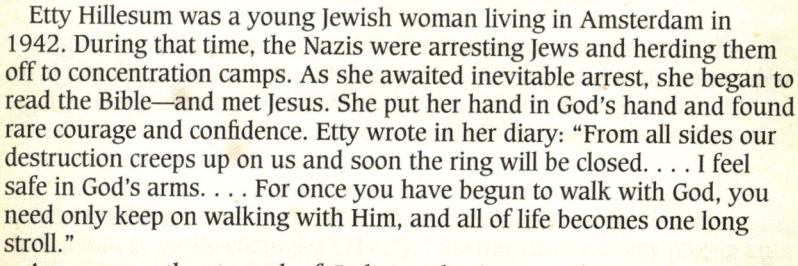

Etty Hillesum was a young Jewish woman living in Amsterdam in 1942. During that time, the Nazis were arresting Jews and herding them off to concentration camps. As she awaited inevitable arrest, she began to read the Bible—and met Jesus. She put her hand in God's hand and found rare courage and confidence. Etty wrote in her diary: "From all sides our destruction creeps up on us and soon the ring will be closed. . . . I feel safe in God's arms. . . . For once you have begun to walk with God, you need only keep on walking with Him, and all of life becomes one long stroll."

As we sense the strength of God's everlasting arms beneath us (Deuteronomy 33:27), we can walk through life with confidence, holding the hand of our unseen Companion. —VG

AUGUST 16

It is good to be near God. —Psalm 73:28

Roy was a gentle, quiet man who sought no recognition and occupied himself solely with his Father's will. His was a heavenly perspective. As Roy often said, "We are but sojourners here." When he passed away, friends reminisced over Roy's influence. Many spoke of his kindness, selfless giving, humility, and gentle compassion. He was, for many, a visible expression of God's love.

At the assisted-living facility where his father lived out his final days, Roy's son gathered up two pairs of shoes, a few shirts and pants, and other odds and ends—the sum of Roy's earthly goods—and delivered them to a local charity. Roy never had what some would consider the good life, but he was rich toward God in good deeds. —DHR

MAY 18

If we walk in the light, as he is in the light, we have fellowship with one another. —1 John 1:7

Physical exercise may help us fight off infection. A workout puts our body in a condition similar to what happens at the onset of a fever—it helps the body fight off infection with higher temperatures. First John 1 and 2 indicate that good spiritual exercise is beneficial to the health of our soul. To ward off sin, we must "walk in the light as he is in the light" (1:7) and obey Jesus each day.

Disobedience cools our spiritual temperature. Fellowship with God and other believers is neglected. If we have a lukewarm faith (Revelation 3:16), we're not taking advantage of the defense mechanisms necessary to fight spiritual infection. The right exercise program is one of faith and obedience. It is essential to spiritual health. Walk with Jesus, and you'll truly be walking for your health. —MD

AUGUST 15

Kiss his son, or he will be angry and your way will lead to your destruction. —Psalm 2:12

Flying from Tampa to Chicago in January, we were bathed in brilliant sunshine at 37,000 feet. But thick clouds covered O'Hare. "Take a good look at the sun," someone joked. "You won't see it again until April!" Christians also invite people to "look at the Son"—the Son of God—and trust Him for salvation.

In the wilderness, the Israelites were attacked by fiery serpents. God had them fashion a brass serpent and raise it on a pole; whoever was bitten could look up and be saved. "Just as Moses lifted up the snake in the wilderness," Jesus said, "so the Son of Man must be lifted up, that everyone who believes may have eternal life in him" (John 3:14–15). No wonder the psalmist exclaimed, "Kiss his son!" —RD

MAY 19

We live by faith, not by sight. —2 Corinthians 5:7

"When I Think of Heaven" is a tract written by Joni Eareckson Tada, who is paralyzed from her neck down because of a diving accident during her teenage years. Joni admits that thinking about heaven isn't always easy, especially since we have to die to get there, unless Jesus returns first! She says God works through trials to help us focus our minds on heaven. As one who lives, travels, and ministers in a wheelchair, Joni writes confidently about heaven: "I'll be fantastically more excited and ready for it than if I were on my feet. Suffering gets us ready for heaven. Heaven becomes our passion."

The apostle Paul knew that kind of passion. We groan for heaven, he said, because we long to be with our Lord forever (2 Corinthians 5:6–8). —JY

AUGUST 14

People go to their eternal home. —Ecclesiastes 12:5

"Be sure to call when you get home. I want to know you arrived safely." Does that sound familiar? Having bid farewell to dear ones—committing them to the Lord's keeping—we eagerly await the word that assures us they've arrived at their intended destination. What a welcome thing it is when the phone rings and a voice exclaims, "We're home—safe and sound!"

Our loved ones who've been summoned to their eternal home don't need to send such word back. We know from Scripture that their journey from earth to glory was a safe one. Even as Jesus told the dying thief, "Today you will be with me in paradise," certain is the quick and happy arrival of every departed Christian in heaven. —RD

MAY 20

I rejoiced with those who said to me, "Let us go to the house of the LORD." —Psalm 122:1

While visiting a city in Moldova, Charlie VanderMeer was impressed by the dedication of the Christians. For a Sunday morning service, 1,500 people showed up—and only 25 of them arrived by car. Most walked through the snow—and some changed buses up to five times to get there. Then, they turned around and did it all again for the evening. Amazed at the dedication of these people, Charlie wondered, "Would we go to church if we had to do that?"

The Christians of Moldova, like the people David wrote about in Psalm 122, were willing to go to great lengths to worship God. As believers, we worship the same living God. Let's go to the house of the Lord with the same joy and eagerness. —DB

AUGUST 13

Now the Berean Jews were of more noble character than those in Thessalonica, for they received the message with great eagerness and examined the Scriptures every day to see if what Paul said was true.
—Acts 17:11

   The Pony Express ran nineteen hundred miles, from Missouri to California, in ten days. Forty men, each riding fifty miles a day, dashed along the trail on the best horses the West could provide. To conserve weight, clothing was light, saddles small and thin, and weapons left behind. Yet each rider carried a full-sized Bible! Why? Because the Scriptures were deemed standard equipment. God was important to these people, and they recognized the need of searching and obeying the Word.

   God has provided us the standard equipment of His revelation, the Bible. Like the noble Bereans, may we receive this important "love-letter" with eagerness. —HGB

MAY 21

He who was seated on the throne said, "I am making everything new!"
—Revelation 21:5

As I walked past a new luxurious high-rise apartment in downtown Grand Rapids, I heard a passerby say, "If I could just get that top-floor apartment, I could live there forever." But think about that possibility. Imagine spending eternity *anywhere* in this fallen earth. Buildings deteriorate. Neighborhoods change. Nations collapse. World conditions worsen. To capture the very best of this world and hold on to it forever would be to miss something far better—the glorious wonders of heaven and the new earth.

No believer in Jesus Christ should ever want to spend eternity on this earth as it is. We have a greater hope. Only when we see Jesus should we ever want to say, "I could live here forever!" —DCE

AUGUST 12

We are always confident and know that as long as we are at home in the body we are away from the Lord. For we live by faith, not by sight. —2 Corinthians 5:6–7

D. L. Moody wrote of times when "we dwell in high altitudes of grace, and heaven seems very near." But that's not always true. It's often the exception to the rule. Most of the time, "clouds and fog caused by suffering and sin" obscure our view of coming glory.

The Christian's final destination is certain, whether or not we see it clearly. In stormy seasons, believers can ask God to renew their determination to press on, to "live by faith, not by sight." The apostle Paul experienced distress and suffering, but he was confident that "the one who raised the Lord Jesus from the dead will also raise us" (2 Corinthians 4:14). The key to victory in the Christian life is to "live by faith"! —RD

MAY 22

I will come back and take you to be with me that you also may be where I am. —John 14:3

When death invades our lives, we need a sanctuary—a place of safety that gives us a glimmer of hope against an oppressive backdrop of sorrow. This was never more clear to pastor John Claypool than in the days following the death of his young daughter. Claypool said he found enough strength and courage to keep going in John 14. He was confident that Jesus had prepared a better place for his daughter—and that she was with the Lord. "The only thing that keeps me going," he said, "is the promise that my daughter is in the arms of Jesus."

Our Savior is preparing a better place for all who have put their trust in Him. It's a reality that gives us the comfort we need to face the death of someone close. —DB

AUGUST 11

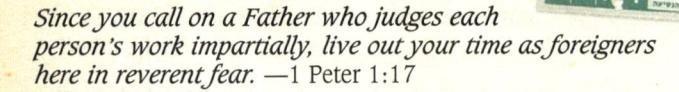

Since you call on a Father who judges each person's work impartially, live out your time as foreigners here in reverent fear. —1 Peter 1:17

During the Great Depression, many American men became tramps. They hopped freight trains to travel, slept in empty boxcars, and earned a little money working odd jobs. Sometimes they begged. Having lost the security of home, they wandered aimlessly. Pilgrims, like tramps, may be without the comfort and protection of a home—but pilgrims know where they're going. The Christian is that kind of wayfarer! So Peter gives the exhortation, "Live out your time as foreigners here in reverent fear" (1 Peter 1:17). Why? Because he is a pilgrim on his way to heaven, not an aimless wanderer! The Lord is preparing you and me for eternity, and everything we do is full of significance. Let us live responsibly, with our destination in view. —HVL

MAY 23

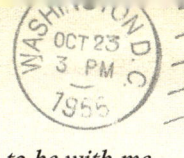

"Father, I want those you have given me to be with me where I am, and to see my glory, the glory you have given me because you loved me before the creation of the world." —John 17:24

As a boy, I was thrilled whenever I saw pictures of the majestic buildings in our nation's capital. Of special interest was the Capitol building. To me, its dome symbolized America at its best. When I finally had the privilege of visiting Washington, D.C., my heartbeat quickened as we approached. At last I was seeing what I had dreamed about for so long.

An even stronger anticipation is my longing to see heaven, a place of "many mansions." Although we don't have many details, we know enough to make our hearts yearn for heaven's beauty. And with that hope is the expectation of seeing Jesus. When we enter that glorious place and are ushered into the presence of the Savior, the experience will be vastly more wonderful than anything we've ever dreamed of. —PVG

AUGUST 10

Do not offer any part of yourself to sin as an instrument of wickedness, but rather offer yourselves to God as those who have been brought from death to life; and offer every part of yourself to him as an instrument of righteousness. —Romans 6:13

Back in the horse-and-buggy days, a couple was traveling a narrow, dangerous stretch of road. The woman was nervous, and in her fright grabbed one of the reins. Her husband calmly offered the other. "No," she cried, "I don't want them both! I could never manage that animal alone!" "You must make a choice," he replied. "It's either you or me. We can't both drive the horse." She quickly surrendered full control to her husband, and they journeyed safely onward. The situation is much the same for Christians. We must yield all to God so He has full command of our daily activities. Insistence on our own way will only lead to heartache and failure. Turn the "reins" of your life over to Christ! —RD

MAY 24

Just as you received Christ Jesus as Lord, continue to live your lives in him. —Colossians 2:6

Walking is just one step away from falling. That's why venturing out on two unsteady legs can be frightening to a very young child. Yet children keep at it until walking becomes second nature. This is similar to learning to "walk" as a Christian. We put our faith into practice one step at a time. Paul urged believers to live by faith so they would become firmly established in their walk with Christ (Colossians 2:6–7). We do that by focusing our thoughts on Him: what He has done, what He is doing now, and what He will do for us.

Walking with Christ may sometimes be frightening, but it is the only way to make progress in our spiritual development. Are you walking with Him today? —DD

AUGUST 9

The LORD became angry with Solomon because his heart had turned away from the LORD, the God of Israel, who had appeared to him twice. —1 Kings 11:9

Leaving his winged friends in flight, a wild duck landed on a farm to mingle with tame ducks. Food was plentiful, and he stayed the summer. When autumn came, he heard the wild ducks heading south, but though he wanted to join them, his added weight prevented much flight. As time went on, he paid little attention to his former companions.

Followers of God can also be lured into complacency by losing their high ideals. King Solomon began with a sincere desire to be wise and righteous, but compromised himself by marrying pagan women. Let's submit ourselves fully to the Lord, renewing our commitment daily, staying true to His high purpose for our lives. If you're tempted to join the wrong crowd, remember the parable of the duck! —HVL

MAY 25

For we live by faith, not by sight.
—2 Corinthians 5:7

We often wish we could see what lies around the corner in life. Then we could prepare for it, control it, or avoid it. My ten-year-old granddaughter Emily and I were boiling eggs for breakfast. As we stared into the boiling water and wondered how long it would take, Emily said, "Pity we can't open them up to see how they're doing." We began talking about other things we would like to see but can't—like tomorrow. Too bad we can't crack tomorrow open, we said, to see if it's the way we would like it.

Because Jesus has promised to care for us every day—and that includes tomorrow—we can live by faith one day at a time (Matthew 6:33–34). Emily and I decided to leave tomorrow safely in God's hands. Have you?
—JY

AUGUST 8

For he was looking forward to the city with foundations, whose architect and builder is God. —Hebrews 11:10

Called by God to leave his home and travel to an unknown land, Abraham is a picture of all believers who also journey to a blessed new destination. The patriarch realized he'd been directed to more than just an earthly territory. With the eye of faith he saw that the Lord had chosen him to be an heir of salvation. He would eventually dwell in an eternal city "whose architect and builder is God."

F. B. Meyer says that Abraham went in faith, "not only leaning on the promises but leaning on the Promisor!" This truth is also our strength. We go forward with sealed orders, but we advance confidently, recognizing the best this world can offer will never compare with the joys of heaven. —HGB

MAY 26

He who testifies to these things says, "Yes, I am coming soon." Amen. Come, Lord Jesus. —Revelation 22:20

Nearly two thousand years ago Jesus said, "I am coming quickly." Since then, some have wrongly tried to predict when He will return. Others have scoffed. Was Jesus wrong? Did something happen that He didn't foresee? Of course not! We view time from the perspective of our own brief life span. But to the eternal God, "With the Lord a day is like a thousand years, and a thousand years are like a day" (2 Peter 3:8).

Jesus told His disciples that God had not given them specific information about "times or dates" (Acts 1:7). He wanted them to live in an attitude of expectation. The Lord's any-moment return is no cause for date setting but for watchful expectation. Let's serve Him in every aspect of our lives, and one day we'll hear Him say, "Well done, good and faithful servant" (Matthew 25:21). —HVL

AUGUST 7

Then they came to Elim, where there were twelve springs and seventy palm trees, and they camped there near the water. —Exodus 15:27

After the people of Israel crossed the Red Sea, they entered a vast, parched wilderness. They found an oasis, but its water was bitter. So God told Moses to cast a tree into the pool, and "the water became fit to drink." They were heartened by God's intervention and further encouraged when their next stop was an ideal encampment at Elim. There, they enjoyed twelve good wells of water in a grove of shade trees.

Israel's experience is analogous to the Christian's. Moses' tree pictures the cross of Christ, taking the bitterness out of our deepest trials. And along life's way God gives blessing to compensate for our trials. In the reviving shade of Elim's seventy palms, our testimony is renewed and victory attained. —HGB

MAY 27

Your word is a lamp for my feet, a light on my path.
—Psalm 119:105

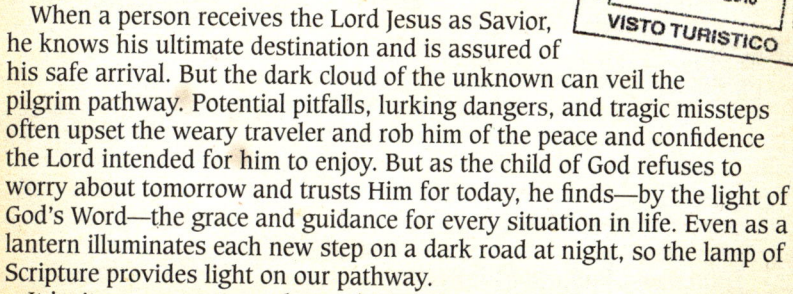

When a person receives the Lord Jesus as Savior, he knows his ultimate destination and is assured of his safe arrival. But the dark cloud of the unknown can veil the pilgrim pathway. Potential pitfalls, lurking dangers, and tragic missteps often upset the weary traveler and rob him of the peace and confidence the Lord intended for him to enjoy. But as the child of God refuses to worry about tomorrow and trusts Him for today, he finds—by the light of God's Word—the grace and guidance for every situation in life. Even as a lantern illuminates each new step on a dark road at night, so the lamp of Scripture provides light on our pathway.

It isn't necessary to see beyond what the Lord reveals. Follow His leading. There's always enough light for each step! —RD

AUGUST 6

My times are in your hands; deliver me from the hands of my enemies, from those who pursue me. —Psalm 31:15

In a European art gallery is a painting that puzzles at first glance. It portrays a solitary figure, bowed down with fear, running across a bleak landscape. Overhead hangs an ominous cloud. But upon closer inspection you notice the cloud is in the shape of a hand . . . and the meaning of the picture becomes clear. The lonely, frightened traveler, seeking refuge from a storm, is actually under the protective care of God.

So it is with everyone who believes in Jesus. The trials and storms do not come by chance. They are planned and sent by Him. And if we look to Him in faith, we will see that the cloud always takes the shape of His sheltering hand. Never fear! —PVG

MAY 28

Enoch walked faithfully with God; then he was no more, because God took him away. —Genesis 5:24

Have you ever wondered what it would be like to go through life without giving God a thought? How lonely and frightening it would be! As children of God through faith in Jesus, we not only have a wonderful future but we also can experience a deep, settled peace as we enjoy communion with Him. From morning to night, we can find comfort and assurance in fellowship with God.

An unknown poet described what it means to walk with God: "Begin the day with God, kneel down to Him in prayer; / Lift up your heart to His abode and seek His love to share. / Open the Book of God and read a portion there, / that it may hallow all your thoughts and sweeten all your care." May we all have that kind of fellowship with God! —RD

AUGUST 5

I am torn between the two: I desire to depart and be with Christ, which is better by far. —Philippians 1:23

Countless believers through the centuries have found that when their earthly lives came to an end, a glorious way opened before them. Near death John Bunyan said, "Weep not for me, but for yourselves. I go to the Father of our Lord Jesus Christ." John Wesley said just moments before he left this earth, "The best of all, God is with us." And the apostle Paul declared, "For to me to live is Christ and to die is gain."

Life's highway may be smooth, and it may seem to stretch on indefinitely. But there is a barricade ahead marked "Death." Will your road end there? Receive Christ to take the highway to heaven. —DD

MAY 29

We fix our eyes not on what is seen, but on what is unseen, since what is seen is temporary, but what is unseen is eternal. —2 Corinthians 4:18

When Pat Kelly played for the Baltimore Orioles, his manager was fiery Earl Weaver. Weaver kept his mind on one thing—winning baseball games. One day Kelly said to his manager, "Weave, it sure is good to walk with Jesus." "That's nice," the manager replied, "but I'd rather you would walk with the bases loaded."

That exchange is a good example of the difference between two views of life—the temporary and the permanent. When we have the first, we can become preoccupied with the things of this earth. With the permanent view, however, we recognize the importance of getting ready for eternity by trusting in and living for Jesus Christ. How would you label your outlook? Is it temporary or permanent? —DB

AUGUST 4

I have fought the good fight, I have finished the race, I have kept the faith. —2 Timothy 4:7

An old-time railroad engineer was late on a run. He prayed for safety and asked, "Lord, help me bring her in on time." He couldn't gain a second on the climb up the mountains, but the train flew down the other side. As he pulled into his destination, he saw he was exactly on time. Moments later, a man tapped a cane on the locomotive's window. "A good run, sir! A very good run!" the railroad president shouted. "That meant more to me than anything in this world," the engineer said. "When I make life's last run and pull into the Great Terminal, I hope I'll hear Christ say, 'A good run, sir! A very good run!'"

Are you anticipating the Savior's "well done"? —PVG

MAY 30

Give careful thought to the paths for your feet and be steadfast in all your ways. —Proverbs 4:26

In *Pilgrim's Progress*, Christian and Hopeful are walking the King's Highway to the Celestial City. The path, once smooth and easy, becomes rough and hard. Then they come to an attractive place called Bypath Meadow. Soon the new path becomes rugged and steep. A terrible storm breaks overhead. Exhausted, Christian and Hopeful lie down and fall asleep. Suddenly, the Giant of Despair drags them to Doubting Castle and throws them into a dungeon. Hurt and confused, they despair. They begin to pray. Christian remembers that he's carrying in his pocket a key called Promise. He unlocks the door, and soon they are on the King's Highway again.

Are you doubting? Filled with despair? Come back to Jesus. Confess your sin. Accept His promise of forgiveness. Return to the right path. —DCE

AUGUST 3

God is able to bless you abundantly, so that in all things at all times, having all that you need, you will abound in every good work. —2 Corinthians 9:8

In the center of Bath, England, stands a stone marker in honor of the city's medicinal waters that have blessed so many. Grateful citizens had the monument inscribed with the following words: "These healing waters have flowed on from time immemorial. Their virtue is unimpaired, their heat undiminished, their volume unabated. They explain the origin, account for the progress, and demand the gratitude of the City of Bath."

How like the grace of God! It too is an endless stream of freely flowing, health-giving water that never cools and never fails. From beginning to end, the Christian life is a matter of grace. Grace alone explains the origin of our salvation and accounts for our progress in sanctification. Thank God for His boundless grace! —PVG

MAY 31

Let us run with perseverance the race marked out for us, fixing our eyes on Jesus, the pioneer and perfecter of faith.
—Hebrews 12:1–2

A man decided to try a barrel-like amusement ride that tilted and turned. He said to a friend, "I'll show you how to walk through without falling." When he entered the barrel, it started turning. Before long, he lost his balance, fell, and began to roll around inside. When the ride finally stopped, he emerged embarrassed. The ride operator said, "Do you see that shiny thing hanging at the far end of the barrel? If you'd kept your eye on that instead of looking at your feet, you could have walked right through."

Similarly, on the topsy-turvy pathway of life, we can easily be made to stumble. But the author of Hebrews told us how to avoid falling: by "fixing our eyes on Jesus." —PVG

AUGUST 2

For to me, to live is Christ and to die is gain.
—Philippians 1:21

Author Henry Durbanville told of an elderly lady in Scotland who wanted to see Edinburgh. She was afraid to take the train, though, because it would go through a long tunnel to reach the city. But circumstances arose that forced her to travel to Edinburgh. Worn out with worry, the woman quickly fell asleep on the train. Upon awakening, she found she was already in the city. Durbanville commented, "It is even so with the dying saint. He closes his eyes on earth, passes into what he thinks of as the tunnel of death, and opens them immediately in the celestial land." Dying may seem dark and foreboding. But for the Christian it's only a brief transition into the glorious presence of the Savior! —RD

JUNE 1

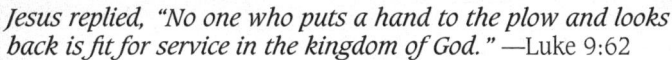

Jesus replied, "No one who puts a hand to the plow and looks back is fit for service in the kingdom of God." —Luke 9:62

The Australian coat of arms pictures two creatures, an emu (a large flightless bird) and a kangaroo. They were chosen for this honor because of one common characteristic—neither can move backward. If an emu, with its big, three-toed feet, tries to go backward, it will fall over. And the kangaroo is kept from going backward by its long tail. They can only move forward, and so portray the spirit of Australia.

As believers in Christ, we should resolve to always move forward spiritually. As we read the Scriptures, we can look for commands to obey and principles to put into practice. When we do, in the Holy Spirit's power, we'll ensure that we move only forward in our walk with the Lord.
—DCE

AUGUST 1

So do not be ashamed of the testimony about our Lord or of me his prisoner. Rather, join with me in suffering for the gospel, by the power of God. —2 Timothy 1:8

Some things that appear dangerous are actually less hazardous than the alternatives. Airline travel, for instance, is many times safer than automobile transportation. The same is true in our journey through life. Following the Lord may seem perilous. It must have appeared that way to those who deserted the apostle Paul when he was imprisoned for speaking on Christ's behalf. But Paul had really chosen the best way, a path that involves suffering but is ultimately safer than the alternatives. He could declare, "I know whom I have believed, and am convinced that he is able to guard what I have entrusted to him until that day" (2 Timothy 1:12).

Commit yourself to the Lord no matter what. It's the safest way to go. —MD

JUNE 2

It was I who taught Ephraim to walk, taking them by the arms; but they did not realize it was I who healed them. —Hosea 11:3

One day, I noticed a small child learning to walk. The little fellow would take some tottering steps, and plop—down he'd go. His dad would pick him up and he'd start again, arms flailing. After a few feet, he would tumble again. I wondered how long it would take him to walk without falling.

God said that He taught the Israelites to walk. He took their arms and supported them. Through the Holy Spirit, He does the same for us when we trust Jesus. Our first steps of faith are like that boy's. We soon fall. Then the Lord picks us up, and we start again. Once more we stumble. But our heavenly Father is always there to set us on our feet. —DCE

JULY 31

The LORD will watch over your coming and going both now and forevermore. —Psalm 121:8

The Choice Gleanings calendar beautifully described how we can face each day with confidence when it described how "the camel's day begins and ends in the kneeling position." At sunrise, the camel kneels to receive its load, carefully chosen by its master. At night, the camel kneels again for the master to lift the burden away.

All of us bear some burden (Galatians 6:5). It may be the small cares of everyday duties, or our concern for the welfare of unsaved loved ones. Others labor under the burden of disease, infirmity, weakness, or disability. What comfort and encouragement to know that God watches over our "coming and going"—all our steps from sunrise to sunset. And He knows exactly the load we can handle. —DD

JUNE 3

Not that I have already obtained all this, or have already arrived at my goal, but I press on to take hold of that for which Christ Jesus took hold of me. —Philippians 3:12

After his death in 1807, the wife of English painter John Opie said she never saw him satisfied with his art. She reported that many times he would cry out, "I never shall be a painter as long as I live!" C. H. Spurgeon said that this artist's dissatisfaction "was a noble despair, such as is never felt by the self-complacent daubers of [the ordinary], and it bore the panting aspirant up to one of the highest niches in the artistic annals of his country." Spurgeon added that, for the Christian, "the self-same dissatisfaction with present attainments is a potent force to bear [him] onward to the most eminent degree of spirituality and holiness."

The Christian walk must ever be an upward walk. —RD

JULY 30

My Father's house has many rooms; if that were not so, would I have told you that I am going there to prepare a place for you? . . . Store up for yourselves treasures in heaven. —John 14:2; Matthew 6:20

A couple was traveling abroad, intending to build a house upon their return. When they found beautiful pictures, statues, or vases, they purchased them and sent them ahead to await their arrival. When placed in their new home, these items would stir happy memories and contribute to their future enjoyment. All of us can do the same for our heavenly home. The kind deed that made a rare picture in somebody's life, the little sacrifice that blossomed into joy, the helpful friendship—all these we shall find again as treasures in heaven.

Jesus has gone ahead to "prepare a place" for us. But we can participate now. He instructed us to show Christian love to others. That's how we store up "treasures in heaven." —RD

JUNE 4

You intended to harm me, but God intended it for good to accomplish what is now being done, the saving of many lives. —Genesis 50:20

Bible teacher Warren Wiersbe tells the story of a boy who was leading his younger sister up a steep mountain path. The climbing was difficult, with many rocks in the way. Finally, the girl, exasperated by the hard climb, said, "This isn't a path at all. It's all rocky and bumpy." "Sure," her brother replied, "but the bumps are what you climb on."

If anyone ever faced obstacles, the biblical Joseph did. His brothers hated him. He was sold into slavery. He was falsely accused and thrown into an Egyptian prison. Yet he continued to trust in the Lord and walk by faith. Rather than causing him to stumble, hardships were steppingstones in his service for God. Remember, "bumps are what you climb on." —DCE

JULY 29

When they came to the place called the Skull, they crucified him there, along with the criminals—one on his right, the other on his left. —Luke 23:33

Journeying through Appalachia, my wife and I were captivated by the hills and mountains. But our most vivid memory is the repeated whisper of three crosses along the road. A pastor preached that one cross portrays a thief dying *in* sin, another a thief dying *to* sin. But the center cross speaks of the Redeemer dying *for* sin. All humanity falls into two categories—rejecters who die *in* sin, and receivers who die *to* sin.

Having received Christ, how do we die to sin? Yielding to God's Spirit, we speak truthfully, deal with anger daily, engage in honest work, check the first shoots of bitterness, and forgive as God has forgiven us. By dying daily to our sins, we experience the fullness of eternal life. —DD

JUNE 5

The night is nearly over; the day is almost here. So let us put aside the deeds of darkness and put on the armor of light. —Romans 13:12

In Michigan's Upper Peninsula, the woods are extremely dark at night. While staying at a cabin there, my family and I noticed that when we first stepped outside we couldn't see anything. Soon, though, our eyes grew accustomed to the blackness. When we had been away from the light long enough, we began to feel at home in the dark. But there were still dangers in the shadows.

I'm sure you see the spiritual parallel. When we're saved, we know the light. Occasionally, though, we're tempted to go back into the world's darkness. If we don't stay in God's light, we face a subtle danger. The blackness of sin doesn't seem so bad anymore. But the going is much safer when we stay in the light. —DCE

JULY 28

[Jesus] bore our sins in his body on the cross.
—1 Peter 2:24 (NASB)

Near the top of a church tower in Norway stands the figure of a lamb. When the church was being built, a workman fell from a high scaffold and landed on a lamb just as a flock of sheep passed below. The lamb broke his fall and was crushed to death, but the man was saved. The statue stood as a reminder.

John the Baptist described Jesus as "the Lamb of God, who takes away the sin of the world" (John 1:29). Peter said the full weight of our sins fell upon Jesus (1 Peter 2:24). And Paul explained, "God made him who had no sin to be sin for us" (2 Corinthians 5:21). On the cross Jesus took the punishment for our sin upon himself. Have you been saved by the Lamb? —MRD

JUNE 6

These were all commended for their faith.
—Hebrews 11:39

In a letter to his son Eduard, Albert Einstein wrote, "Life is like riding a bicycle. To keep your balance you must keep moving." We can apply this wise counsel to the Christian life. Many believers by faith keep moving ahead through painful and trying circumstances. But when they experience a personal moral failure, they lose their balance and fall. Their feeling of unworthiness of God's forgiveness may then keep them down, and they no longer move ahead in their spiritual life.

The Bible gives many examples of those who experienced serious personal failure, including Abraham, Jacob, and Moses. Despite their failures, we are told: "These were all commended for their faith" (Hebrews 11:39). Have you lost your spiritual balance through a sinful choice? Repent and follow the God of second chances once again. —DF

JULY 27

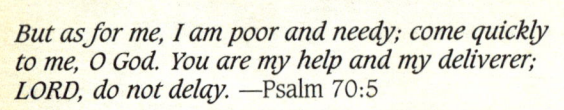

But as for me, I am poor and needy; come quickly to me, O God. You are my help and my deliverer; LORD, do not delay. —Psalm 70:5

Fishermen of France's Brittany peninsula would often say this prayer as they set out to sea: "Keep us, our God, for Your ocean is so wide and our boat is so small." It's a prayer that all Christians might offer on the sea of life.

At times our challenges and difficulties threaten to overwhelm us. We sense our weaknesses and inability to overcome them. We feel like crying out to the Lord in the words of the psalmist, "I am poor and needy. . . . You are my help and my deliverer" (Psalm 70:5). In our "small boats," on a "wide ocean," we can trust our God to protect us even in the worst of storms. Let's ask Him to keep us today. —RD

JUNE 7

When he has brought out all his own, he goes on ahead of them, and his sheep follow him because they know his voice. —John 10:4

A missionary had to walk through unfamiliar territory at nighttime. Going through the darkness with his guide just ahead, he looked down and noticed he couldn't see the pathway. The guide changed directions so often the missionary feared they were lost. He cried out, "Where's the way?" The guide turned and said calmly, "I am the way. There's no path here; just follow my steps and we'll arrive safely." The missionary did, and they reached their destination.

As we journey through life, we too must learn to trust our Guide. As weak, helpless sheep who can't find the path ourselves, we can trust the unerring guidance of the Good Shepherd. He searches out the safe way for us; even better, He goes on ahead! —HGB

JULY 26

Cast your cares on the LORD and he will sustain you.
—Psalm 55:22

    Charles Spurgeon loved to tell about his grandfather, a minister, who was very poor. His one cow had died, and his ten children were without milk. His wife asked, "What will we do now?" "I cannot tell," he said, "but I know what God will do. We must have milk for the children and He will provide for us." The next morning a man brought Spurgeon's grandfather a gift of twenty pounds from the ministers' relief fund, even though help had not been requested. Those men knew nothing about Spurgeon's cow, but God did.

    As God's children, we can either carry our cares ourselves or give them over to the Father. Life's journey is a lot easier if we learn to cast rather than carry. —PVG

JUNE 8

*In you our ancestors put their trust;
they trusted and you delivered them.*
—Psalm 22:4

On a road trip, our GPS led us off the Interstate, through a small city, and back to the highway. I was baffled. Why take us off a perfectly good road? That got me thinking about detours in life. We're on a smooth path. Then for some reason, God redirects us into unfamiliar areas—an illness, a crisis at work, an unexpected tragedy. We don't understand why.

Abraham faced a mysterious detour when God said, "Go from your country, your people and your father's household" (Genesis 12:1). He must have wondered why, but he trusted God's purpose.

A GPS may err. But we can trust our unfailing God to guide us through mysterious detours, leading us exactly where He wants us to go. —DB

JULY 25

The apostles said to the Lord, "Increase our faith!" —Luke 17:5

Millions are afraid to travel by air. A conscious fear of crashing is rarely the problem; it's the fear of losing control once the plane leaves the ground. Similar fear may occur when people put themselves in God's care. Carried a long way from "solid ground," trusting an invisible Lord can be frightening.

Jesus' disciples experienced a crisis when He said they'd have to reach unimaginable levels of forgiveness (Luke 17:3–5). Responding to their lack of faith, He said only a little obedient trust put the power of heaven at their disposal (v. 6). That's the key. When we learn what Christ wants, we must take the first step of obedience. Then He'll give us the strength to do what He wants us to do. —MD

JUNE 9

Your path led through the sea, your way through the mighty waters. —Psalm 77:19

The Channel Tunnel opened in 1994, nearly two centuries after it was first proposed. Today the 31-mile passage beneath the English Channel allows thousands of people, cars, and trucks to travel by train daily between England and France. People had always sailed the Channel until this new route was completed.

In Exodus 14:10–22, God planned an unexpected route for His people. Faced with death, either from Pharaoh's army or drowning, the Israelites nearly panicked. But God parted the Red Sea and they walked through on dry land. God can create roads where we see only obstacles. When our way is uncertain, it's good to remember what He has already done. God specializes in miraculous pathways—pointing us to His love and power.
—DCM

JULY 24

He has granted us new life to rebuild the house sof our God and repair its ruins. —Ezra 9:9

If you choose to turn up Luis Brandeis Street in Jerusalem's Jewish Quarter, you'll encounter the Tiferet Yisrael Synagogue—or what's left of it. Employed as a strategic defense site during the 1948 Arab-Israeli War, the structure was dynamited into rubble. In 2014, reconstruction finally began on Tiferet Yisrael Synagogue. As city officials set a piece of the ruins as the cornerstone, one of them quoted from Lamentations 5:21. In that heart-rending elegy for Jerusalem, the prophet Jeremiah prays, "Restore us to yourself, LORD, that we may return; renew our days as of old."

Our lives, too, may seem in ruins. Troubles of our own making and conflicts we can't avoid may leave us beaten, bowed, and broken. But we have a Father who understands. Gently, patiently, He clears away the rubble, repurposes it, and builds something better. —TG

JUNE 10

Little by little I will drive them out before you, until you have increased enough to take possession of the land. —Exodus 23:30

There's a story about a little boy with a small shovel. He was trying to clear a pathway through deep, new-fallen snow in front of his house. A man paused to observe the child's enormous task. "Little boy," he inquired, "how can someone as small as you expect to finish a task as big as this?" The boy replied confidently, "Little by little, that's how!" And he continued shoveling. In Old Testament times, God had promised a land to His people. The obstacles facing Israel as they thought about claiming the land—the many powerful people groups already there—must have seemed insurmountable. But He didn't ask them to do it all at once. "Little by little" is the strategy for victory. —JY

JULY 23

We are confident, I say, and would prefer to be away from the body and at home with the Lord.
—2 Corinthians 5:8

    Famed British leader Winston Churchill (1874–1965) specified that his funeral should begin with the playing of "Taps," the traditional military signal played at the end of the day—or the end of life. But when the service ended, attendees were startled to hear trumpets play "Reveille," the call that awakens troops for a new day.
    The end of life is in some ways like the end of a day. The journey is long. We get tired. We long for our labors to be finished. Ahead lies the night of death. But, thank God, morning is coming! A wonderful life lies just ahead for weary Christian travelers. To be absent from the body is to be present with the Lord forever (2 Corinthians 5:8). —DCE

JUNE 11

Encourage one another and build each other up.
—1 Thessalonians 5:11

As we traveled, my friend was getting frazzled. At the airport, she fumbled with her identification and couldn't find her reservation confirmation. A patient ticket agent helped her at the self check-in. After receiving her ticket, she asked, "Where to next?" The agent smiled, pointed at me, and said, "Stay close to your friend."

The apostle Peter wrote to believers who needed one another as they suffered for their faith. He urged them to "love each other deeply," pray, and offer hospitality (1 Peter 4:7–9). In other passages, we're encouraged to comfort each other (2 Corinthians 1:3–4) and build each other up in love (1 Thessalonians 5:11). When life gets difficult and we're frazzled, staying close to Christian friends will help us get through. —AC

JULY 22

Do everything without grumbling or arguing.
—Philippians 2:14

   I was seated behind two small children who were not happy about being on a plane. Their complaints filled the cabin. Just before takeoff, a flight attendant stopped, smiled, and said, "What's all this squawking up here?" After charming the fussy kids for a few minutes, the attendant bent down and whispered very seriously, "I must remind you, this is a non-squawking flight." The little ones became unbelievably quiet, making everyone feel better. It's a long journey when you sit in the squawking section.

   I'm sure God wants to remind me that He wants this to be a non-squawking day. If we banished complaining, how would it affect our family and friends? What about our ability to share the Word of life with others? —DCM

JUNE 12

*In their hearts humans plan their course,
but the LORD establishes their steps.*
—Proverbs 16:9

A high school singing group arrived at a nursing home for a Thursday concert . . . though the folks at the home were expecting them *Friday*. But if the group could set up fast, they could sing twenty minutes until a memorial service for one of the residents began. The chorale hurriedly organized and sang, and the son of the man who had died heard them. When they finished, he asked if they'd sing at his dad's service. They gladly agreed and ministered hope and truth to those attending. God used these young people powerfully—because of a secretarial error. But was it a mistake?

If we're doing God's will, we'll be in the right place. Wherever we are, we can point people to Him. —DB

JULY 21

I consider everything a loss because of the surpassing worth of knowing Christ Jesus my Lord. —Philippians 3:8

One of baseball's all-time greats made a revealing admission. "For years I ate baseball, I slept baseball, I talked baseball, I thought baseball, I lived baseball," Ty Cobb said. But, he added, "When you get beyond those years of playing professional baseball, you can't live on baseball."

We can devote our energies to a vast multitude of pursuits. But in the end nothing will prove sufficient except the one lasting purpose the apostle Paul described: "For to me, to live is Christ" (Philippians 1:21). Knowing Christ—trusting Him, abiding in fellowship with Him, serving Him—is the one driving purpose that saves life from being little more than a monotonous march of meaningless days. Life becomes a joyful journey with our Savior and Friend. —VG

JUNE 13

If anyone . . . sees a brother or sister in need but has no pity on them, how can the love of God be in that person?
—1 John 3:17

Friends of ours were traveling, and having car trouble several states away. Short on money, they called to let us know—but there wasn't much we could do except pray and trust that God would watch over them. As they sorted things out from a fast-food restaurant booth, a man approached with bags of burgers and fries. "God told me I should give you some food," he explained.

How many times have we seen God send help on the way? On the flip side, how many times have we felt the urge to help someone and balked at the notion? We are God's hands on earth—created both to receive help and give it. Do you know someone who needs help on the way? —DB

JULY 20

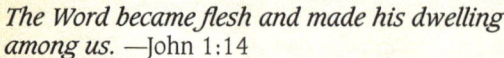

The Word became flesh and made his dwelling among us. —John 1:14

A girl in Africa gave her teacher a beautiful seashell. The teacher was touched, knowing the girl had walked many miles to find it. "You shouldn't have traveled so far," she said. Smiling, the girl replied, "The long walk is part of the gift."

This girl probably didn't realize she was conveying a truth about Jesus. He gives the gift of eternal life to all who believe in Him (Romans 6:23), and that gift began with a journey. He left heaven for earth, taking humanity upon himself (John 1:14). He walked the road to the cross, where He bore our sin and penalty. When I gratefully say to Him, "You shouldn't have," I imagine Him replying tenderly, "The journey is part of the gift." —DCE

JUNE 14

You greatly rejoice, though now for a little while you may have had to suffer grief in all kinds of trials. —1 Peter 1:6

Have you ever taken one of those vacations? You planned to go somewhere you knew you'd love, but on the way you had so many difficulties you wondered if the journey was worth it. Car problems. Traffic delays. Getting lost. Sick kids. Irritable fellow travelers. You knew the destination would be great, but the trip was anything but smooth. Yet you kept pressing on because you knew it would be worth the trouble.

That's a picture of the Christian life. Those who have trusted Jesus as Savior are on a journey filled with difficulties, setbacks, tragedies, and obstacles. Yet we know that an indescribably great destination is in our future (1 Peter 1:4). Troubled today? Look ahead. Heaven will be worth the trip. —DB

JULY 19

The path of the righteous is like the morning sun, shining ever brighter till the full light of day.
—Proverbs 4:18

During bad weather I exercise on a treadmill. But it's boring! When the odometer says I've walked a mile, I've actually gone nowhere. Life without God is like that. "Generations come and generations go" (Ecclesiastes 1:4). The sun rises and sets day after day, year after year (v. 5). Rivers flow into the sea, but it's never full (v. 7). Like these natural phenomena, life is always moving but never arriving. Then comes death. People without God know they will soon be forgotten.

How different for those who know God! Yes, they sometimes experience monotony and difficulty, but they're on a journey instead of a treadmill. When we admit our sins and receive Jesus as Savior, He transforms our lives from dreary to meaningful. —HVL

JUNE 15

The LORD watches over all who love him.
—Psalm 145:20

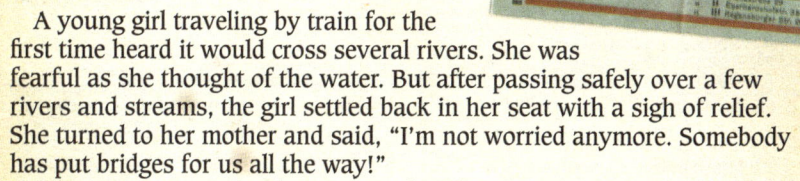

   A young girl traveling by train for the first time heard it would cross several rivers. She was fearful as she thought of the water. But after passing safely over a few rivers and streams, the girl settled back in her seat with a sigh of relief. She turned to her mother and said, "I'm not worried anymore. Somebody has put bridges for us all the way!"

   When we come to the deep rivers of trial and the streams of sorrow, we too will find that God in His grace "has put bridges for us all the way." We don't need to fall into hopelessness and anxiety. Instead of worrying about what's ahead, we can trust the Lord to be there to care for us.
—HGB

JULY 18

Whatever you do, work at it with all your heart, as working for the Lord, not for human masters.
—Colossians 3:23

Centuries ago, Irish believers reminded themselves of God's presence in every activity of life. They would pray in the morning: "Thanks to Thee, O God, that I have risen today to the rising of this life itself." Many ended their day saying, "I lie down with God, and God will lie down with me."

Their practice challenges us to perform everyday tasks "as working for the Lord, not for human masters" (Colossians 3:23). The apostle Paul also wrote, "Whether you eat or drink or whatever you do, do it all for the glory of God" (1 Corinthians 10:31). Paul's words embrace everything—eating breakfast, doing dishes, sharing conversation, operating a computer. Everything is to be done for God, with an awareness of His presence. —VG

JUNE 16

Do not be like the horse or the mule, which have no understanding but must be controlled by bit and bridle.
—Psalm 32:9

An experienced guide was leading tourists through dangerous gorges and ice fields in the Swiss Alps. While on a wide detour for safety, one weary tourist decided to take a shortcut and left the pathway. The guide chased the man, tackled him, and dragged him back to the path. Then he explained that the snow the tourist intended to walk over was a thin crust of ice covering a giant crevasse. The "shortcut" would have meant a deadly plunge.

Our guide, Jesus, sometimes leads us on detours that seem unnecessary. If we leave the pathway of obedience, He may use painful means to drag us back to spiritual safety (Hebrews 12:3–11). He has His reasons—and we can thank Him for tough love! —VG

JULY 17

[You] have put on the new self, which is being renewed in knowledge in the image of its Creator. —Colossians 3:10

Over the centuries, many attempts have been made to restore damaged and timeworn masterpieces of art. Some attempts went well and some actually damaged works of genius, including at least two paintings by da Vinci. In his letter to the Christians at Colosse, Paul described a restoration process that's impossible in the art world: The restoration of God's people. "You have taken off your old self with its practices and have put on the new self" (Colossians 3:9-10). This is spiritual renewal by our God, who created us and gave us new life in Jesus. His forgiveness brightens the colors of our lives.

The canvas of our lives is in the skilled hands of our Lord, who knows what He designed us to be. No matter how sin-damaged we may be, there's hope for restoration. The Master Artist is at work within us. —DCM

JUNE 17

In all this you greatly rejoice, though now for a little while you may have had to suffer grief in all kinds of trials. —1 Peter 1:6

Long ago, before passenger trains had electric lights inside, a Christian was traveling on a route with several long tunnels. As he talked with a fellow believer beside him, the train was suddenly enveloped in darkness. The other man had traveled the line often. "Cheer up," he said. "We're not in a sack—there's a hole at the other end!"

That's good to remember when we pass through trials like the apostle Peter described. Frequently, without warning, we can go from the brightness of godly joy to a state of gloom. But God's children are never "in a sack"—there's always "a hole at the other end!" Our "tunnel experiences" are merely God's way of getting us through mountains we could never scale ourselves. —HGB

JULY 16

Everyone is but a breath, even those who seem secure.
—Psalm 39:5

At age sixty-four and in good health, British novelist William Somerset Maugham wrote his autobiography. "An occasional glance at the obituary columns," he explained, "suggests that the sixties can be very unhealthy." Maugham would live another twenty-seven years.

Whatever our age, it's good to occasionally review our lives. Are we achieving our goals? Becoming the kind of people we aspire to be? Far more important is whether we're becoming the people *God* wants us to be. Because life is fleeting (Psalm 39:5), we're wise to make the most of our limited days.

We can't change the past. But from here on, we can prayerfully lay hold of grace and fulfill God's will for our lives. We have this moment—make the most of it! —VG

JUNE 18

*Be still before the LORD and wait patiently for him;
do not fret when people succeed in their ways, when they
carry out their wicked schemes.* —Psalm 37:7

In 1832, a French engineer was traveling the Mediterranean. When another passenger became sick with a contagious disease, their ship was quarantined. To pass time, the engineer read about a man who had studied the feasibility of a canal connecting the Mediterranean and Red Sea. The experience led the engineer to plan the Suez Canal, which was completed under his leadership in 1869. That quarantine proved immensely valuable to the engineer—and the world.

Likewise, Christians sometimes undergo "spiritual quarantines" to prepare them for further usefulness to God. It may be an illness, injury, or unemployment. In every situation, God draws His people aside so they can know Him and His purposes better. —PVG

JULY 15

*When I am old and gray, do not forsake me, my God,
till I declare your power to the next generation.*
—Psalm 71:18

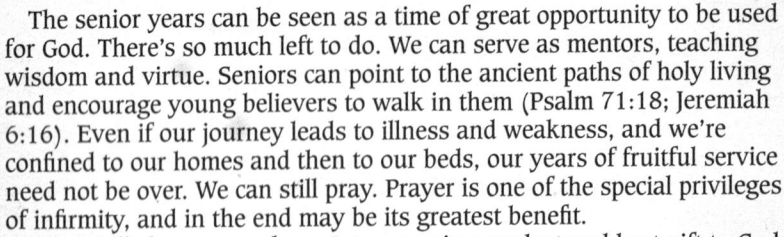

The senior years can be seen as a time of great opportunity to be used for God. There's so much left to do. We can serve as mentors, teaching wisdom and virtue. Seniors can point to the ancient paths of holy living and encourage young believers to walk in them (Psalm 71:18; Jeremiah 6:16). Even if our journey leads to illness and weakness, and we're confined to our homes and then to our beds, our years of fruitful service need not be over. We can still pray. Prayer is one of the special privileges of infirmity, and in the end may be its greatest benefit.

Above all else, we can love. Love remains our last and best gift to God and to others. —DHR

JUNE 19

Our citizenship is in heaven. And we eagerly await a Savior from there, the Lord Jesus Christ.
—Philippians 3:20

President Theodore Roosevelt went on a safari in Africa. When he returned, a missionary—retiring after forty years of service in a jungle village—was on the same ship. Cheering throngs greeted Roosevelt at the dock, but nobody welcomed the missionary. Momentarily, the man felt sorry for himself. "When a president comes home after a hunting trip, hundreds come out to greet him," he thought. "But Lord, when one of your missionaries comes home after a lifetime of service, no one is there to meet him." Immediately, the Lord seemed to whisper, "But, my son, you are not home yet."

Do you sometimes feel like that missionary? Read today's Scripture again. Someday you'll receive the real welcome. —DD

JULY 14

By faith Abraham, when God tested him, offered Isaac as a sacrifice. —Hebrews 11:17

My wife was scheduled for surgery. As a Christian, I couldn't rely solely on good odds for a favorable outcome. Might God take her? It could happen! For faith to be strong and true it must be tested—to the point of being willing to give up our most cherished loves. Abraham's faith was put to the ultimate test. The command to sacrifice Isaac seemed pointless, yet for the crisis to be real the command had to be given and Abraham had to take it literally. In his heart, he did offer up Isaac (Hebrews 11:17).

Faith tested can bring great inner turmoil, but God's design is to perfect it and to reward it with a fuller knowledge of himself. That's worth any crisis. —DJD

JUNE 20

Because Jesus lives forever, he has a permanent priesthood. Therefore he is able to save completely those who come to God through him, because he always lives to intercede for them. —Hebrews 7:24–25

An elderly woman was traveling by train for the first time, going from Montreal to the far west. Being hard of hearing, she wanted to be alerted when her station was called, so she asked the conductor to notify her when they reached Kamloops, British Columbia. "I don't go that far," the man replied. "You won't reach Kamloops for three days, and neither I nor the conductor who takes my place goes through. Ask the one who boards at Calgary."

As Christians, we too are on a long journey. We've never gone this way before. The route is unknown to us, and we want to be sure of reaching our destination. But we have a Conductor who accompanies us right through to the end. —PVG

JULY 13

This brother of yours was dead and is alive again; he was lost and is found. —Luke 15:32

In his fascinating book *Orthodoxy*, G. K. Chesterton tells of leaving what he thought was the Christian faith, only to find the real thing later. To illustrate his spiritual journey, Chesterton describes the absurd scene of planting a British flag on a foreign island, but then discovering it's actually the coast of England. Raised in a lifeless "Christian" church, Chesterton left his nominal faith. But later he doubted the atheistic assumptions that had led to his unbelief. He discovered the truth he'd missed before. He returned "home," much like the wandering teen in Jesus' parable of the prodigal son. At times we all feel the tendency to wander from the One who redeemed us. But our loving Father watches and waits for our return. —DF

JUNE 21

Enoch walked faithfully with God; then he was no more, because God took him away. —Genesis 5:24

People who take the upward way to eternal life (Matthew 7:14) have the Lord as their companion. The patriarch Enoch is a shining example of one who enjoyed that relationship. He lived in an age of violence and apostasy, when people's thoughts were "evil all the time." But by his holy life, he maintained an intimate fellowship with the Lord—and had his name added to the book of Hebrews as a hero of faith. Because he "walked faithfully with God," this man was given a special blessing: Instead of dying, he was taken directly to glory.

So, what about us? Are *we* going God's way? There are joys of communion to be found if we, like Enoch, learn to travel with God! —HGB

JULY 12

If you think you are standing firm, be careful that you don't fall! —1 Corinthians 10:12

    I was sailing along on my rollerblades when suddenly the wheels on my left boot began wobbling. Seconds later, I was down on the asphalt. Just like that, I had a broken finger and nasty cuts on my face. That made me much more cautious on rollerblades. I take every precaution to avoid going down again.

    Falling isn't good. But for anyone who has stumbled in life, something positive can result—if the fall leads to a more careful way of living. Paul admonished, "If you think you are standing firm, be careful that you don't fall!" (1 Corinthians 10:12). Believers do fall. But if you've stumbled in life's journey, there's hope. Ask God for guidance, for He "upholds all who fall" (Psalm 145:14). —DB

JUNE 22

The righteous person may have many troubles, but the LORD delivers him from them all. —Psalm 34:19

After some heartbreaking experiences, a godly missionary was asked how he remained cheerful through adversity. He replied, "Suppose someone sent me on a journey, warning me that I would come first to a dangerous river crossing and then to a forest filled with wild beasts. I would be pleased when I actually encountered these obstacles, because they would prove I was traveling the right road. That's also true in the Christian life. The Lord told His disciples that they could expect tribulation. So when difficulties come, I find encouragement—I know I'm walking the narrow path of God's choosing."

If you're suffering affliction, know that the pathway to glory is often surrounded by thorny trials. But take courage—you're on the right road home! —HGB

JULY 11

Believe in the Lord Jesus, and you will be saved. —Acts 16:31

In a personal evangelism course I taught, I asked students to write the story of how they came to faith in Christ. It struck me how different each journey was. Some were saved out of drugs and immorality. Others were church attenders who met Christ after years of biblical instruction. Conversions vary. The apostle Paul had a crisis encounter with the Savior that turned him from persecutor to preacher (Acts 26). In contrast, Timothy was quietly nurtured in the Scriptures from childhood, resulting in his salvation experience (2 Timothy 3:14–15). No two faith journeys are identical. But each has the common element of turning to the Lord in faith to be saved from sin and to receive a new heart. What's your story?
—DF

JUNE 23

For the LORD watches over the way of the righteous, but the way of the wicked leads to destruction. —Psalm 1:6

A bewildered man drove down a street half asleep, not noticing that all the arrows along the route pointed the opposite way. He was stopped by a policeman who asked, "Where do you think you're going?" The man answered, "I don't know for sure, Officer, but I guess I'm late. Everybody else is coming back!"

Ignoring signs on a one-way street can cause a serious accident. But the consequences of going the wrong direction in life are far worse. Many miss the warning signs God has erected, but the wise accept God's salvation and travel the pathway of life. People who trust God can anticipate with joy their deliverance from the power of death. The Lord will watch over their way . . . forever! —HVL

JULY 10

I waited patiently for the LORD; he turned to me and heard my cry. —Psalm 40:1

I've struggled to understand something I heard as a young Christian: "God can't steer a parked car." I took that as a challenge to shift my life into motion, and then God would guide me in the right direction. It's an interesting thought, but not always the way God works. Occasionally, He wants us to stay "parked." At times in the wilderness, God kept the Israelites in one place. He led them by a cloud, and when it stayed still, the Israelites "did not set out" (Numbers 9:19).

If you feel stuck, like you're just spinning your wheels in your service for God, keep your heart open to His leading. Then you'll be ready to shift gears when you hear Him say, "Let's go." —CHK

JUNE 24

Those who suffer according to God's will should commit themselves to their faithful Creator and continue to do good. —1 Peter 4:19

When we board a plane, we place ourselves in the hands of the captain and crew, trusting them for a safe, comfortable flight. The pilot is briefed on the weather conditions, and jets have radar to scan the skies during the flight. In this confidence, passengers can relax even though they don't know what lies ahead.

So it is with the Christian. We don't know all that the future holds, but we should relax in confidence that God will direct our passage perfectly through the storms of life. We can say with Job, "He knows the way that I take; when he has tested me, I will come forth as gold" (Job 23:10). We can always trust God to give us a "safe" ride. —RD

JULY 9

He will wipe every tear from their eyes. There will be no more death or mourning or crying. —Revelation 21:4

Suffering from cancer and a grueling medical regimen, pastor Dan Cummings was tired. After two weeks of treatment in Texas, he longed to get home to Michigan. Dan blogged, "Today is far better. . . . Will fly home on the weekend to continue treatment." Dan did return home, but his journey on earth soon ended. He went to be with God—whom he loved with all his weak body and mighty spirit. Viewing his blog days later, "Today is far better" jumped out at me. I smiled through tears knowing that Dan was now experiencing life that is truly "better by far" (Philippians 1:23).

Someday we who claim Jesus' name will also go where there is "no more death or mourning or crying." —CHK

JUNE 25

You should not be surprised at my saying, "You must be born again." —John 3:7

Once when crossing the border into Canada, I was asked a series of questions. "Where were you born?" "Where are you going?" "How long are you staying?" The experience reminded me that all of us are making a trip from one "country" to another, and the "border" is crossed at the moment of death. When we reach that border, the answer to just one question will be of prime importance. You will not be asked, "Where were you born?" but rather, "Have you been 'born again'?"

Jesus said, "No one can see the kingdom of God unless they are born again." In other words, only those who have trusted Christ will go to heaven. Are you traveling by God's grace toward the heavenly country? —RD

JULY 8

Do not be afraid; do not be discouraged.
—Deuteronomy 31:8

The Lake Michigan waves were high, splashing onto the pier as I followed a young family out to a lighthouse. I overheard the girl say, "Daddy, please walk beside me and hold my hand at this scary part." Life can be scary for adults too: Loss of loved ones. Financial troubles. Health problems. Carrying these heavy burdens, we long for a strong hand to keep us steady and secure.

As Joshua took over Israel's leadership, Moses reminded him of God's help in tough times. "The LORD himself goes before you and will be with you," Moses said. "He will never leave you nor forsake you. Do not be afraid; do not be discouraged" (Deuteronomy 31:8). When life gets scary, hold onto God's strong hand. —AC

JUNE 26

Suffering produces perseverance; perseverance, character; and character, hope. —Romans 5:3–4

How slow do snails go? One study clocked them at 0.00758 miles per hour—or forty feet in one hour. Although snails move at a "sluggish" pace, one virtue they possess is perseverance. The great preacher Charles Spurgeon wryly observed, "By perseverance the snail reached the ark."

According to the apostle Paul, perseverance is a key component of character development. He explained that "suffering produces perseverance" (Romans 5:3). And upon that building block go character and hope (v. 4). The original Greek word translated *perseverance* means "steadfastness, constancy, and endurance." It was used of believers who endured in their faith despite many painful trials. Have setbacks slowed you down to a snail's pace? Be encouraged. God doesn't ask for a fast finish, only persevering progress. —DF

JULY 7

The statutes of the LORD are trustworthy, making wise the simple. —Psalm 19:7

British auto technicians found a surprising use for certain foods. They built a race car that runs on vegetable oil and chocolate. The fuel propels the car to 135 mph.

The Bible also describes surprising energy from a food. After God used Elijah to defeat Baal's followers at Mount Carmel, the prophet fell into depression. So God sent an angel with some heavenly food, and the effect was remarkable: "Strengthened by that food, he traveled forty days and forty nights until he reached Horeb, the mountain of God" (1 Kings 19:8).

We need food to sustain our physical lives, but we also need nourishment for our spirits. God's Word is "sweeter than honey" (Psalm 19:10) and feeds our souls. Take time to "eat" it. —DF

JUNE 27

The Lord's message rang out . . . everywhere.
—1 Thessalonians 1:8

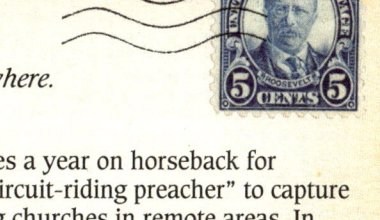

Francis Asbury rode six thousand miles a year on horseback for decades. He introduced the Methodist "circuit-riding preacher" to capture the American frontier for Christ, planting churches in remote areas. In 1771, when Asbury arrived in the colonies, there were about six hundred Methodists in America. Forty-five years later, there were two hundred thousand! Asbury's strategy reflected the apostle Paul's approach. To the church he'd planted in Thessalonica, Paul wrote: "The Lord's message rang out from you not only in Macedonia and Achaia—your faith in God has become known everywhere" (1 Thessalonians 1:8).

The "circuit-riding preacher" is no more, but each of us has a "frontier" mission field of friends, relatives, and neighbors. Who in your life needs to hear the good news? —DF

JULY 6

*He lifted me out of the slimy pit, . . .
he set my feet on a rock.* —Psalm 40:2

Not long ago, I passed a milestone: twenty years of keeping a spiritual journal. Here are some benefits I've received: I see that progress and failure are both part of life's journey. I'm reminded of God's grace when I read how He helped me find solutions to problems. I gain insight from past struggles that help with issues I currently face. And, most important, journaling shows me how God has faithfully worked in my life.

Many of the psalms are like a spiritual journal, often recording how God has helped in times of testing. Journaling may be useful to you too. It can help you see more clearly what God is teaching you on life's journey and cause you to reflect on His faithfulness. —DF

JUNE 28

With the Lord a day is like a thousand years, and a thousand years are like a day. —2 Peter 3:8

In 1896, H. G. Wells published *The Time Machine*. Its protagonist traveled millions of years into the future, finding a world grown cold and dark and the last remnants of life awaiting extinction. Sickened, he returned to the time of his origin to report his anguish.

The biblical view of the future is very different. God is Lord over time itself: "With the Lord a day is like a thousand years, and a thousand years are like a day" (2 Peter 3:8), and we can be optimistic because He will replace our world with a new one. There, we'll experience fellowship with our Creator forever in a place where "there will be no more death or mourning or crying or pain" (Revelation 21:4). —DF

JULY 5

Physical training is of some value, but godliness has value for all things. —1 Timothy 4:8

At New Year's, many resolve to take better care of themselves—to exercise, eat right, lose weight. Paul says, "Physical training is of some value" (1 Timothy 4:8), so I struggle to stay fit. But I know that my body is fading.

It's better to pursue godliness, which holds promise for this life and the life to come. Godliness may sound dull, scary, or unattainable, but it is simply self-giving love—caring more for others than we care for ourselves. We grow more loving (and lovely) by sitting at Jesus' feet, since He is love (1 John 4:8). Life is a journey into love, and there's nothing so beautiful as a godly soul. Physical exercise is good, but there is something far better: love. —DHR

JUNE 29

There is a way that appears to be right, but in the end it leads to death. —Proverbs 14:12

My daughter was coming home from college, and before she left, I sent her an e-mail directing her to take a different route than usual. Why? A few weeks earlier, my wife and I had been delayed by construction on the regular road. Parents must provide alternate routes in life as well. They've observed the wrong paths they or others have traveled, knowing those roads lead to delay or danger. Jesus Christ is the alternate route that leads children away from the struggles they'll face on other roads.

The right route starts with the Via Dolorosa—the way of the cross—through salvation (John 14:6), directed by God's Word (Psalm 119:105), including Jesus as a traveling companion (John 8:12). It's the ultimate alternate route. —DB

JULY 4

God is our refuge and strength, an ever-present help in trouble. —Psalm 46:1

I've written articles and a book on life's losses, and I've been privileged to meet many fellow strugglers along life's journey. We know the losses that knock us off our feet—a death in the family, a child who walks away from God, a physical or mental setback. Yet I've discovered what musician Jeremy Camp made clear in the song "Understand," which he wrote after his wife died: "God is our refuge and strength, an ever-present help in trouble" (Psalm 46:1). That's reason enough to get up again. Camp recognized he could continue, because "I know You understand it all."

When trouble knocks us down, look up to God. He understands and cares. We can trust Him to help us back to our feet. —DB

JUNE 30

Where, O death, is your sting? —1 Corinthians 15:55

My old friend Bob was vigorously pedaling an exercise bike, staring at a blood pressure monitor on his finger. "What are you doing?" I asked. "Looking to see if I'm alive," he grunted. "What would you do if you saw you were dead?" "Shout hallelujah!" he replied with a smile.

I've caught many glimpses of Bob's great inner strength: patient endurance through his physical decline, and faith and hope as he approaches life's end. Death has lost its power to tyrannize him. Who can find peace and hope—even joy—in dying? Only those who are joined by faith to the God of eternity and who know that they have eternal life (1 Corinthians 15:52, 54). —DHR

JULY 3

My only aim is to finish the race and complete the task the Lord Jesus has given me—the task of testifying to the good news of God's grace. —Acts 20:24

The words *always* and *never* hold much hope. I'd like to think I could *always* be happy and life would *never* fail me. But reality says otherwise. So, good as the words sound, they come up short—except in the promises of Jesus' presence.

"I am with you always," Jesus told His disciples (Matthew 28:20). "Never will I leave you; never will I forsake you," Hebrews quotes Jesus as saying (13:5). The apostle Paul assured believers that after death, "we will be with the Lord forever" (1 Thessalonians 4:17). When today is scary and the future looks hopeless, the assurance of Jesus' never-failing presence provides comfort and courage for living. Best of all, when this short life ends, we will *always* be with Him. —DCM

JULY 1

You are to love those who are foreigners, for you yourselves were foreigners in Egypt. —Deuteronomy 10:19

Dietrich Bonhoeffer risked his life every day he stayed in Nazi Germany, but he stayed nonetheless. As a pastor he held clandestine worship services and resisted the evil Hitler regime. Bonhoeffer penned *Life Together*, a book on hospitality as ministry. He taught that every meal, task, and conversation was an opportunity to show Christ to others—even under great stress. He put his principles to the test when he was imprisoned.

God ministered to the Israelites leaving Egypt and instructed them to imitate Him by loving and hosting strangers and widows (Deuteronomy 10:18–19). We too are empowered by God to serve Him by serving others. Who around us seems lonely or lost? Trust God to enable you to share hope and compassion. —RK

JULY 2

As iron sharpens iron, so one person sharpens another. —Proverbs 27:17

Social networks add to the ways we can receive and give spiritual guidance. But it's also valuable to meet face-to-face with mature believers for mentoring. "Elisha . . . set out to follow Elijah" (1 Kings 19:21); Paul mentored Timothy as a "true son in the faith" (1 Timothy 1:2). Moses urged parents to teach their children "when you sit at home and when you walk along the road, when you lie down and when you get up" (Deuteronomy 6:7). Jesus also illustrated how to mentor: "He appointed twelve that they might be with him and that he might send them out" (Mark 3:14).

These passages show the value of meeting face-to-face, in various settings, so we can sharpen one another spiritually (Proverbs 27:17). —DF